OPTIONS

TRADING FOR

BEGINNERS

DISCLAIMER

Table of Contents

The Basics of Options Trading

For many people, the first thing to touch on is what exactly options are. Here, we'll go into detail on what options trading is, along with some critical examples that can help you.

Options at the Core

Let's go to the very basics of options trading. Options are essentially contracts that give the investor a chance to buy or sell securities, such as an index or commodity, at a fixed price within a fixed period of time. So, the investor can buy or sell the security at that price irrespective of the actual trading price. He can also do so any time within the fixed period.

Buying and selling options are done within a market, and from there, these trades are done on contracts for various securities. If you buy an option, it allows you to buy shares later on, and they are called "calls". If you sell these shares later, it's called "put" options.

So let's take an example where you have a house that is worth $1 million, and you then are given the option to buy the house at 800K over the next 3 months. So you pay a 2% fee of this to the seller for the option itself. 2% of the house is 20000 dollars of course, and you simply pay that for the option. So you have the house essentially as an option to buy within the next 3 months.

Now, let's say that three months have passed, and now you can choose whether or not you want to buy the house, or sell the house. In this, you're the buyer of the option, so you're the one who chooses whether or not you want to buy the house, and the one who is selling the house is, of course, the seller. Of course, you have to pay the 2% options fee regardless. So, if you after a few months want to buy the house and from there, if it increases, you can buy it at a much smaller margin than what it may be.

So, let's say the home value increases to 110000. You buy it at 80000 as per the contract. From there, it can be sold again in order to net a 280K profit (300K price increase – 20K fee). This is something that you should definitely act upon. It's used in real estate investing too.

But, let's say that you end up seeing the house depreciate over time, and now, unfortunately, after 3 months it's $700,000, which is 100K less than what you were prompted to pay for it. You should at this point choose not to buy the house, and while you do lose the options fee, it's not much. Because after all, losing 20 grand is much better than losing 100 grand, right?

Options are essentially the option to buy something, and you can choose whether or not you want to invest in this or not (after a certain period of time).

But are they the Same as Stocks?

Nope. That's the short answer. But the long answer is because they aren't representing the part of the company that you have owned. Instead they're basically contracts of different investments, and for many people, they are better because you can walk away at any point.

With stocks, if you invest in it, unfortunately, you're stuck in it until you cash out, or you sell it to someone else. That means that there is more risk there.

However, when you buy and sell options, the trader or the investor does not have to invest in the stock at the end of the options period if he does not want to. Options are usually considered derivative securities, which entails that the price is derived from another value in the assets, or other underlying instruments. They are less risky than stocks, as long as you use these correctly.

With options trading, you will have to pay an options fee. So even if you do not end up investing in the stock, it'll need to be paid.

Investors use these because they are bets on whether something will go up, down, or hedge, and we'll go into deeper details on what all of that means later.

More Examples

Let's take a look at a couple more examples of different types of options. Let's talk about stock options because this is one of the areas where beginner investors look at.

So, let's say you have stock XYZ that's at a certain number. Let's say you can buy that stock for 50 grand, and that's the option. So you could get that stock for 50 grand and let's say that option expires at the end of 3 months. You agree to buy this stock, and then a 2% fee, which is a grand. You then put down 1000 dollars on that, and you watch it.

Now let's say that after 3 months, this company does something super awesome, and from there, you notice their profits markedly increase. It ends up increasing to 150K in the stock share, and you're like "of course I'll take that share" and you decide to do that. That's an example of the stock actually increasing, and you totally buy that option from another. That means you're netting a 99K (100K profit – 1 K fee) profit, which is pretty killer, and you can from there sell the shares of that stock to others to net even more money. That is a contract that you can utilize.

But, let's now look at a second scenario. Let's say that you see the company tank. Which sucks, but that does happen when bad decisions are made, and everyone makes poor choices. It happens, but that means that the stock is going down, and it falls down the tubes. It only has a value of 10 grand now, which means it's a 40K decrease if you choose to buy it. Now if you have faith in this stock somehow that it can magically recover, you might take the risk. But for beginner traders, you know better than that than to stick around with a sinking ship, so you refuse to buy. You lose about a grand, but of course, that's not much compared to how much you could've lost if you actually bought the stock.

That's an example of how it is used in stocks, which is another type of contractual obligation that you can utilize in order to get the full results from this.

Next, let's take more examples of company investments. Let's say you've got this company that you have a chance to buy. Let's say that the going rate for this company is $2 million, but you have an option to buy the establishment for $1.5 million after a 6-month period. This could be a great investment, and you end up putting down the options fee, which let's say is about 5 grand. Now, you watch this company, and it's doing super well. The value of the company increases to 3 million after 6 months. You'd want to jump on that immediately, so you end up investing in this over time. That would be the smart option for this. You end up buying it. But, in a second scenario, let's say there's a problem with the company, and the value goes down. From there, you should from there leave the option, and while you may lose 5 grand, it's definitely better than investing in a million-dollar sinking ship.

And as a final example, let's take selling options on stock shares. You've been investing in general electric for a while, and this stock is increasing, and you might want to potentially set up some calls on your stock. Let's say that you have a stock at 50, and you decide to put an option on there for 55 shares at a dollar. But, let's say the stock doesn't increase and it stays at 50. If that's the case, the option does expire, people won't invest, and oh well, that stinks, but you can make a 3% return on the holdings within the market.

Essentially, it's looking at all of the options and choosing for yourself what will be the best route for you to move going forward.

How and Where to Open an Options Account in the USA

Thankfully, there are a lot of places where you can get options accounts, and here, we'll talk about some of the best types, and how to do so.

The best way to do it is through brokerage firms, but not all of them are equal. Here, we'll talk about some of the best types, and why you should consider each of these.

• **Interactive Brokers**: They have the reputation of low costs, but it can be hard for a lot of people to navigate and is a difficult platform. It has the Trader Workstation platform, which is available in either a downloadable package or even from the website. There is also the IBot, which lets you ask questions in English and get an answer, and if you have more than 100K in assets, you don't need to pay for it the asset fees.

• **Lightspeed**: This is another one that has low per-contract commissions, great software, and LiveVol X doesn't have a monthly charge. But, you will need to have a higher balance in order to open an account, and Lightspeed needs to have a minimum charge of $100 a month on it, and if you're a beginner trader, it doesn't really teach you a lot, so be careful with that.

• **TD Ameritrade:** This is a great one for beginners because it has many educational resources, and you can practice options strategies. It also comes with a ThinkorSwim platform which allows you to choose different strategies that are available. The streaming data is available on all platforms. It does contain higher commissions and contract fees, and high margin rates, and it can be hard to balance it all. However this is probably the best one if you're looking to understand the trades you're doing.

• **Charles Schwab:** This is one of the best for options trading, and you can also get expert insight on how to use it. It does contain options research and tools, education, and also support for your options too. This is actually pretty cheap too, meaning that you can trade these options online for less than 5 bucks and then .65 cents a contract. You can also talk online with reputable traders to help you out.

• **Etrade:** Finally, we have Etrade, which has a low account minimum, and it's one of the most popular due to the fact that the tools are super easy to use. They also offer tiered commission that favors those traders that use it, but this can add up a lot for some of the more casual investors.

You will first and foremost need to know where you can open up an account, and from there, you'll proceed to set up an options account with the brokerage. How to do it is pretty simple, and it involves the following steps:

First, you need to open up a brokerage account. You should compare commissions and look for ones that offer low or no commissions. Read the reviews and learn from mistakes. Make sure to always research the platform.

You should look into whether or not you are going to need a cash account or margin account. Cash accounts will only allow for purchases or opening up positions. If you want to sell options to open up the account without having underlying assets, you need to have a margin account. You should look to see if the brokerage has safe forms of payment, or if it's using third-party payments.

Next, let's say you find the right company that you want to work with, and now, you need to get approval before you begin. The brokerage will look at your submission and from there, set limits on trading based on the experience you have and the amount of money you possess. And of course, each firm has its own requirements for this. If you need help, you can always choose a broker that has extra services to assist you and help you learn the ropes. Remember, you can't write these covered calls without an options account, because this will prevent any risk that may happen. Covered call writing is, of course, selling the right to buy the stock that's there. The buyer, of course, always has this right, not the one that's selling. The stock has to be within the brokerage account, and cannot be sold, or even transferred, while the call is on the able.

At this point, once you get approved, you can start options trading. It is good to have a decent amount of money saved up to begin with. Some of these brokers allow you to start with a low amount of money, but a couple of grand might be a better option for you if you're worried about your hard-earned cash possibly going down the drain.

The difference between Level 0, 1, 2, and 3 Accounts

When you begin with this, you're going to have different account levels. You're going to begin at level 0. most brokers don't classify every option, but for the most part, Level 0 is trading stocks and funds. Each options broker might do it differently, but for the most part, the various criteria are relatively the same.

Level 1 allows you to only do covered calls, along with protective puts. This is more hedging than speculative in nature, and this usually requires the options trader to own the stock underneath it all. Covered calls are used when you're using different call options on these stocks in order to hedge against this small drop in the price on the stock underneath it all. Protective puts are when you put options on there as protection on this stock. Currently, you can't buy these call options or put options without having the underlying stock. So if you want to use put and call options on say, some Apple stock, you got to own it first at this levels.

Level 2 is essentially a step forward, and it allows you to buy the call or put options that are there, on top of what Trading level 1 lets you do. This is where most beginners start at, and usually, this is usually just one singular direction of steps. They simply buy puts or calls without writing them or anything more.. The risk on this is limited in terms of money before you purchase these options as well, so remember that.

Finally, you've got level 3, which is where you trade debit spreads, which are on top of everything that 1 and 2 allow you to do. Debit spreads are essentially strategies that allow you to pay cash on, but credit spreads give you the cash when you put these on. We'll go over different spreads later, where you can write various options to secure a position on the market. Usually, the risk is limited to the money that's paid towards putting these on a spread. However while the risk is limited, it's much more complex than simple calls and put options, and usually, you're going to need more knowledge as an options trader.

Most transactions are typically determined by the trading level, and the experience that you have, along with your net worth. So the more experience that you have, the lower your risk is to both the broker and yourself. Which is why a lot of questions that are on the risk assessment form include how long you've been trading, and the instruments that you're trading with are asked. The richer you are, the more losses you can take on, and you're essentially much lower risk. This is why we stated beforehand that you should make sure that you do take the time to assemble a small nest egg of savings to trade with since it can help you immensely. You will not have to worry about verification or proof of the info provided. But this creates a problem because some of these beginner traders think they can handle some of these larger account trading levels, but that isn't the case.

So how do you increase it? Well, they automatically don't increase. You may need to call up the broker to discuss it with them, and your options broker can look at your track record, and your account size to figure out where you should be placed. Usually, though, level 5 naked calls don't require more than a larger amount of funds and the like to satisfy the requirements. You typically can get into these larger accounts if you have more than 200k in your account or more.

So, don't despair if you start off at a lower level. This allows for less risk between yourself and your broker, and that means you won't have to worry about potentially losing a ton of money.

Volatility and Options Trading

Finally, let's talk volatility. This is a measure of the change and magnitude of the prices of the underlying stock that the option tends to have. Usually, the premium of the option will be higher when the volatility is higher, and if it isn't that volatile, you'll notice the fee will be lower. You should look at the volatility of your options, and from there, you can input the value of this into standard pricing models in order to calculate the market value of these options.

Volatility is worth mentioning since it can impact your options trading either good or bad, depending on what you're looking at. There is the risk/reward consideration, and you need to look at the volatility of this. Most trading platforms will tell you automatically but understanding that at the underlying level is just as important, because it's a concept that can ultimately help you.

Historical volatility and implied volatility will tell you whether or not they are expensive or inexpensive. You may question whether these options are over or under-valued in some ways too, and this will, in turn, relate to the theoretical price that's there versus the market prices that are incorporated into there. You need to understand the volatility of this since it will help determine how much this will change when you do invest in it.

For example, if there is a lot of volatility to the stock underneath it, such as if you're trading a stock option, you're going to realize that with time, it's actually important to invest in this type of stock. That is because it could potentially work out for you. You should (if you notice a stock that isn't very volatile) realize that you may end up losing out on it, especially if you don't see much growth. When you're a beginner, you should consider those that have some volatility to it, but not enough to where it can get overwhelming for you.

We discussed a little bit of these terms and mentioned them in passing, and from here, we'll tell you a little bit about the different definitions of such, and why they matter.

The Call

Call or call options is essentially the option that gives the holder the power, and it doesn't give them the obligation to buy the underlying stock at a price by fixed expiration date. Call options typically give you the right to buy the stock that you want. So, essentially, if you want to buy a stock, you need to put out a call option.

The Put

The put or the put option is essentially a way to give the owner the right to sell a security that's there, which is at a specified price that you're looking to sell it, and within a certain time frame. This contrasts to the call option, which gives the holder the right to buy underlying security that's there at a price before this expires.

Buying

Buying, of course, is the decision to invest money into the option that you're getting. Buying means that you're going to obtain the security that's underneath it all. For example, if you're getting a call option for buying a house at 600K when it's valued at 800K, you'll be paying for that whenever it's over, and you choose to buy and take it, you also can take on a specified number of shares that are there too, for example, if you choose to invest in the option to buy 100 shares of a stock.

Selling

Selling is the flip side of this. If you want to sell X number of shares, you'll take a put option and put it out. That means, if you do choose to sell once the expiration date happens, you'll gain a net sum of money. With buying, you lose a sum of money, but you can always turn around and then sell it once again when the market is right. Essentially, if you're looking to get some money, you sell., If you're looking to invest and put money into something, that is when you buy. Both of which do require money and planning and watching the market for any volatility that transpires.

Underlying Stock

The underlying stock is literally the stock, security, interest rate, currency, commodity, index, or whatever is literally what the option is based on. You essentially base the option on this. A call option on Google stock, for example, gives the one that is holding it the right to purchase the Google stock at that price.

So you have a call option to buy that house at 800K, you're given the right to purchase the underlying security of the house that is there. If you have a put option to sell the house at 800K and choose to use it, well that house will then be sold for that price. It's literally what you're trading underneath the option.

Expiration Date

The expiration date is essentially the last day that you can exercise the right to buy/sell the option. If you have that there, any time on or before this day, the investors will choose what to do with this.

For example, let's say that you have a call option set for 3 months down the road. You can watch the market, and the second you see a jump in your favor, you can choose to use that call, and from there, you pay. At this point, you then have the right to the underlying stock. You can choose what to do with this before the expiration date. If you don't see any chance of it helping you at all, you can choose to then let the contract completely expire, deeming it worthless. Many will hold the expiring contract for as long as they can, making sure they close on it before the final trading day. They can also hold the contract or ask for the broker to buy or sell the asset.

The expiration date is usually the third Friday of the month when it expires. If it falls on a holiday, it immediately goes to the Thursday beforehand. If it passes the expiration date it's invalid, so the last day to trade these is usually the Friday (occasionally Thursday) before it expires. That's why traders decide on their options on there.

In general, the longer the stock has to expire, the longer it has to reach the strike price, and the more time value it has, which we'll talk about.

It's important to understand the expiration date because the concept of time is what's at the heart of giving these options the value that they have. Once the put or the call expires, time value doesn't exist, so once the derivative expires. At that point, the investor won't have any rights that go along with owning the put or call, so remember that.

Strike Price

We mentioned strike price in passing, but essentially this is the price that the derivative contract is bought or sold in this case. This is mostly used for stock and index options. For example, with call options, the strike price is where the security is bought by the buyer up till the expiration date. For those put options, the strike price is the price which can be sold up to the expiration date.

These are mostly used in options trading, and usually, this is a key variable within puts and calls. For example, the buyer of a stock option does have the right to buy the stock in the future at a price. The buyer of this will have the right to sell this. The strike price is one of the most important determinants of the option itself. These strike prices are established initially when they're written, telling the investor what this asset needs to reach before it's in the money.

Before we continue, let's talk about **in-the-money or ITM. That means that the option has a value that's affordable in comparison to the market price. Usually, this allows you to buy it below market** price, and it allows you to sell above the market price, so it may have the option of making a profit.

In contrast, **out-of-the-money means that you may lose out on it.**

The main difference between the underlying price of the stock and the strike price does determine the value of the option. Basically, this will show you how much you're going to gain or lose from this. Buyers of put options will be in the money when the strike price is above the underlying stock, and out of money when the underlying stock is above the strike price.

Premium

The options premium is the income that is received by the investor who writes the contract to another party, and it involves the current price of the contract that has yet to expire, and it's the dollar amount per share. This usually involves 100 shares. It's basically the fee paid by the investor to the owner of the stock.

Writing means selling so it will put this as the income that's on the line with this. Usually, they are quoted, and that is what seller going to make off of this, based on 100 shares.

Time Value

This is the part of the premium that's attributed to the time remaining before it expires. The premium contains the intrinsic value and the time value. The premium is based on both of this, and time value is more of the extrinsic option.

Now for definition, intrinsic value is the calculated or perceived value of the asset, investment, or company. Usually, this is used in the fundamental analysis to estimate the value that the company and the cash flows have. This is used to help understand the amount of profit that's in the contract as well.

Time value is important because the cost of an option is the premium. The options buyer pays this to the seller in order to get the right that's gained by this option. From there, you can choose the option to sell or buy the asset, or just let it expire. The intrinsic value is the difference between the price of the underlying asset, such as the stock, or even the commodity or whatever you're taking out on, and the strike price of this. The intrinsic value of the call as well is equal to the underlying price of this, minus the strike price, and the intrinsic value is the strike price minus underlying. So, the time value is equal to the premium minus the intrinsic value (which is the cost of the strike price minus underlying, or vice versa).

Basically, the amount of money the premium is in excess of the intrinsic value is the time value. So let's say you have a Google stock that's priced at $1,044 for every single share you have a 900-call option, so the option has the intrinsic value of 144 dollars (difference between actual value and option). If the trading (premium) of this is say 97 dollars, then the time value of this is 47, due to the fact that the intrinsic value of that minus the value of the trade itself.

Exercise

Finally, we've got exercising options, which is essential when you exercise or use the different options. Calls and puts allow for the owner to buy the stock at certain prices, and when the holder of such call and put options are in the money when selling or buying, which means that they will make a profit, they will "exercise" this option. Essentially, it means using it.

But, because an option is "in-the-money" it doesn't mean that they will always be in the best interest of the person holding onto it to keep it. Most of the time, the options trader is better off selling the option back at the price of this, because usually, it's higher in some cases than what the intrinsic value. Expiration dates usually will be when someone exercises the options.

So when do you exercise these options? Well, it is usually exercised when the stock price is higher than the strike price, and from there, you should exercise it. Once at this point, you can buy the stock at a lower price, then sell it for higher.

When you exercise a put, you do so at a lower than the strike price, and from there, you can exercise it, sell it back immediately, and then buy it at a lower price. It's essentially using this option, getting the underlying stock underneath, and then choosing whether to hold onto it, or sell it.

Some basic Options Quotes and examples

So let's take two different options quotes that showcase all of these. First, let's go with call options since usually, you're beginning with buying. So you have a stock that you want to buy so you'll have a put option. Let's say that it is 100 shares of Apple stock at a strike price of 10 dollars. The stock is trading at 9 dollars on the market. Let's say that the option allows for you to buy this stock at 10 dollars. Well, it would be silly to buy it, since it's at a much higher level. That means that you shouldn't buy a call option to buy this at 10 dollars since it's trading for lower. But, let's say that the strike price is 8, but it's trading at 9 dollars. Well, you should definitely exercise that option, and it can then be exercised on. If you wait a bit, and then after a bit, it goes down to 7, well you missed your chance. With options trading, it involves getting the option exercised at the correct time, so that you end up profiting off of the trade.

Let's take another example. So you've got a quote board, which shows the call option for XYZ on there, and you find out that it's an option. You will find out that if you were to sell the stock, you could get up to say 20-45 dollars if the value is at .2-.45. The decimals are per 100 shares, so you'll want to consider how you invest it. If the call value is at 1.75-2.00, that means that there is a chance you're going to need to pay for it up to 200 dollars.

If that's the case, you're better off buying the stock than selling it, because the put option is rather weak.

On the flip side, let's say that the call quote is .5-.75, which means 50-75 a share. That's great for buying since it's pretty cheap. Let's say that it's that on August 30th, and you have an options trade that goes for that long. If you notice that there is a good day within the expiry date, it may be worth it to invest in that call options. If you notice that the put quote option is between 3.4-3.8, that means it can be 340-380 dollars for the stock, which is A LOT more than some of the market values are. In that case, it would be in your best interest to exercise that put option and sell it especially if it's before the expiration date.

Reading the way the company is going is very important for you to understand options trading. For example, let's take company XYZ, a trading company that trades currently at 40 dollars a share, so 40 is the strike price, and put options are at $2.00. You expect this company to have the shares go down, and shorted 100 shares of this directly at 40$. Your friend may expect this to go down too, and they get a put options contract of 100 shares for $200.

You wait a bit, and after a bit, it rallies to 70 dollars during the expiration of this, and if you decide to go that route, you can lose 3 grand, and your friend will only lose the 200 and nothing more. But, if the stock falls, you can make a grand from that, and your friend will lose a lot more.

This can be a bit hard to understand initially, but once you get a feel for it, it'll make sense.

Advanced Options Quote: The Options Chain

So let's take an options chain, which is the whole matrix listing of one singular security, showing all of the options contracts. An option chain is a list of all of the calls and the put options that are there based on a specific underlying security, which is stock. It is very important that you read all of this in order to make informed decisions. When you log into your online brokerage account, you can look at the option quotes based on different rows, within the options chain using real-time data.

They typically look like this for some options

Symbol	Last	Strike	Bid	Ask	Chg	% change	Vol	Open interest	Imp. Volatility
MSFT18706C	20180703	75	9.25	12	.5	2.75	8	4	80
MSFT18707P	20180709	78	8.75	10	1	1.25	69	10	120
MSFT18707P	20180709	73	9.10	8	2.5	-1.2	180	80	65
MSFT18708C	20180710	74	8.24	12	-1.0	3.76	604	47	1
MSFT18708C	20180711	76	9.10	11	-2.5	1.9	431	85	55
MSFT18708C	20180710	80	9.5	10	3	.5	11	46	0

At this point, let's take one example. In the table above, you'll see an options chain for Microsoft options.. You will look at the call options. You can look at put options as well. You may notice the different shades that are there, which do mean something. If they aren't shaded, it means that they are "out of the money" so you're losing a profit. Usually, you can get different chains that are there and how they factor in.

When you look at this chain, the first thing you'll notice is the first column list that showcases the different contracts that are out there and a lot of symbols. You'll also notice that each symbol refers to the stock that it belongs to, and then when the options expire. You'll see MSFT, which is a symbol for Microsoft. You'll then see different numbers, such as 180706, which means that it was expiring on July 6th, 2018. You will see a C, which means call, and if you were looking at puts, you would see the P option. You will then see a 007500, which means that the current strike price is that, so 75 dollars in this case.

That's just the first column. Let's now tackle column number two, which is the time in which the last trade of this took place, so it's essentially when it was traded last.

Next, you've got the strike price, which is the price that the owner of the call has the right to buy it until the expiration date. So if it says 75 on there, that means 75 dollars. Let's say that the last time someone made a trade deal was on July 3rd, so it would say on the second column 2018-07-03

The fourth column is the bid price, which is the amount which the buyer is willing to pay for this option. You may look over, and it says, for example, 9.25, which means $9.25.

Next, you've got the asking price, which may be higher, or lower. You may see 12 on there, and that means $12. Reminder that both of these equals 100 shares of stock, so whatever is there is multiplied by 100 shares. That means when you look at this, you multiply all of that by 100. So 12 on there means $120 per 100 shares of stock.

Next you'll see to the right the change in the option, which is the difference between the price option of the day shown, and the previous day. So let's say that it has the price of 12 today when yesterday it was 12.5. That means that it went down by .5 in this case and it will have a minus sign in it.

Then you have the % change column, which means the change in the current price minus the previous days' price. This can be determined by how much or how little it is.

From there you've got the eighth column, which is the volume of the contract, which is the number of particular options traded on that day. If you see 4 for example, you'll see four of them traded on that day.

Then there is column 9, which is open interest, and in turn, is the total number of contracts that are currently outstanding on this. This means that the contracts that have been traded that are yet to be exercised, expired, or closed. Sometimes this number can be small, such as 1, sometimes it can be large, such as 280, and really, it just shows how many have taken advantage of a certain number, and who are still waiting out on this.

Finally, you've got implied volatility, which can go over 100%. This is used to indicate how volatile, or not volatile, a stock's price will or will not be in the future. If there is a lot of volatility, it means that the stock will have larger percentage swings in different direction. If it's low, it means that it won't really change all that much. If you see the number at 0, it means it's going to be like that.

Implied volatility is important for the pricing of these contracts. Typically, those with higher volatility will have a higher premium, and those that are lower will have a lowered premium price to them.

Really, the best thing to do is to look at each column and get familiarized with this. I know that it's a lot to take in, and a lot to understand, but this alone will help you become the best options trader that you can be.

The Covered Calls

Next, let's talk covered calls. You may not know about these yet, or maybe you've heard about them from earlier in this book. It's another super important options trading step, and here, we'll talk about what it means, why they matter, and how they can really help you as an investor.

What is a Covered Call?

Covered calls by definition are essentially a means to help you generate income, especially in the form of premiums. This is done with assets that you've had for a long time. If they're held in a long position, you can then sell these call options, or write them, and generate income.

So if you have longtime asset investments, such as stocks or housing, a covered call is super great. This is good for investors that are neutral or bullish in stocks.

So if you've been holding onto that Disney stock for a long time and want to utilize it to your advantage, this is how.

Covered calls will make you money whenever the stock price increases or stays constant during the time of the contract. You can lose money if the stock price falls too much, and you can still make money if it falls a little bit. It will also protect the investment from decreases in share price value while giving yourself a chance to make some money when the stock price does go flat.

You can also sell these too. And this means you'll get a lot of extra money as you hold the stock, and you can sell it at different prices if it does turn too highly valued. This type of option in particular is valuable in a bearish or flat market.

Examples of Buying and Selling

Next, let's talk about how you sell and buy covered calls. For example, let's say you buy 100 shares of a stable stock from years ago, and it's at $30 a share, which is considered undervalued, and it was paying $1 a year in dividends out of $2 per earnings share. You'll be getting a respectable amount of 3.33% of an increase. The bank has a higher credit rating, and it's growing at a good pace. If you have an investment in this, and it's been doing that for a long time, you'll have some pretty good earnings.

However, you may end up getting a lot more in dividends and is now up to a higher share. If it's higher than it was when you bought it, and the dividend is lower than 2.77% in value due to the price of the stock increasing faster than the dividend growth, there's no new catalyst for more growth or anything like that. It's not something you'd get today if you were looking for new stock. It's a good company, but not worth the value that it is currently.

If you have this stock, you may be keeping it to avoid the capital gains tax, unless you're doing it from a retirement account.

You may choose to keep it for now, and keep collecting the low dividend, with some price appreciation, but it might be overvalued by a lot already, so price appreciation is limited.

This would be a good time to look into selling the covered call, and from there you can sell these options at different strike prices. You may choose to do one at $47, for example, which is above the stock price, and you get a good premium bid. If you sell this at this point, you'll get $94 (2% premium from the buyer), and you'll be obligated to sell all of this at $47 each, for a total for you of $4700. This nets you a pretty hefty sum, provided you do so before the option expires.. If you sell multiple options, you can sell several hundreds of shares.

If it stays under $47, you will probably still have the shares, but then when that expires, you can sell another options contract. You can do this three times in a row, and essentially, you can make money, in this case, up to 3 different option periods, each time making decent cash.

So, pretty much regardless of how you're selling it, you should realize that you're going to win either way. If the stock stays under $47, you'll get to keep the premium, but if it goes over, you will need to sell. It kind of stinks when you have to sell because you won't get the benefits, but you could always go back and rebuy it again during a market change, or just get an all-new stock.

Let's take another example. You have 100 shares of IBM stock, and it currently trades at 100, but you're sure it'll be below 105 for a while. You may sell some call options with a strike price currently at 105. From there, it's $3 a share it controls 100 shares. By selling this, you get the premium of $300 in exchange for the chance that you can sell this at $105 between now and the expiration date, which let's say in this example is in September. You essentially will then wait to see what happens. Let's say that the stock trades at expiration at $103. While the buyer will lose 300, you gain 300 from this, and they're now worth more.

Let's says it goes up to $110, which is higher than what you got. You will have to sell the stock at $105 even if it's valued at 110.

So you gain $500 because you're selling your 100 shares at a profit of $5 each, and you still get to keep that $300 premium, which means you're still making 800 dollars regardless. Covered calls do have the potential to limit the upside profit in exchange for receiving that premium upfront. This can increase as well. If it is traded at 115 at expiration, you'll still make a really good amount of money regardless.

But, what if IBM's stock goes super low, that means that option won't work, and it's worthless. The buyer of the option will have lost $300 regardless, and you'll lose some value in the stock, but you can buffer the premium there. If you have no intent on selling these shares, locking in the loss, you keep the premium and wait for it to bounce back.

So, in essence, covered calls are great for stock that you've just kept around for a long time, and that's why they matter.

The Benefits of This

Well for one, you're essentially preventing yourself from losing out on many sources of income, and that is why it is so important to understand this. They are essentially the safest means to sell.

For starters, you will always have that premium. Regardless of the trade, you are making some cash on your asset, which means that you are going to always win regardless. However, there is also the fact that even if the option becomes worthless, you are still going to end up making some money. On the buyer's end, you are always going to lose out on some money. For the seller, you will notice that you can always turn around and also re-sell these shares if the person decides not to use the option, which is a major benefit of this.

Covered calls are also super safe, which means that you are losing out on a lot less money than other options. It is suitable for almost all types of retirement accounts too because you will not have to worry about paying taxes on this. In this type of trade, if you have an investor selling a call option on the one that they own, this is covered. If you don't have underlying stock, then it's a naked call.

Because options lose their value when they approach the expiration dates, selling these tend to be much more profitable than buying, as you've seen in this example. Covered call works best if you're an investor that has some underlying stock that you've been holding for a long time and ones that you don't expect to increase in the long term. The investor will, in essence, limit their potential in return for a premium that is guaranteed.

So you're always going to get that premium regardless, which means that you're going to make money period.

They are great for investors that are looking to generate additional income for a specific holding. Naked calls, in particular, are more for speculating, and the investor should be very confident in the direction the stock will take. The investor should always have resources on hand to cover these mistakes. With covered calls, the investor will have to sell the stock in a worst-case scenario.

So in essence, if you have a lot of stock that you've just been holding onto, and you don't know what to do with it, then you should definitely consider this option. That's because it provides the most security that you can get from an options trade, and it will turn prevent anything bad from happening.

Because let us face it, the worst you're getting here is that you'll need to sell the stock. However, you are still making a profit while selling the stock.

How to Find the Best Assets for Covered Calls

So your best option for covered calls are well, stocks. These are stocks that know will have some future growth, but not too much. You will be able to keep the premium regardless of whether the price goes up or down.

You want stocks that don't rise too much and instead stays relatively within the same position. Remember that the worst that happens if you have to sell it, but you make money, keep a premium, and you can repeat this. The worst is that you get a premium and not much more.

The three companies that have been good for covered call writing are the following:

• Best buy: This retailer has fended off the threat of e-commerce and still grows

• USPS: It's the biggest package delivery

• American Electric Power: The largest electronic transmission network within the US

All of these stocks are good for those with call options since they can appreciate in value, and you should look to make sure that they contain the following factors:

• Pays a current dividend of 3% or more on this

• Has a recent history of strong share price movement upwards

• Is a sector that's expected to perform well for a long time

You can look for stocks that pay a solid dividend for many reasons, and you can invest in this since you can wait for the stock to appreciate and get paid as well, and you can always reinvest the money into different stocks in order to compound the rate of return. Stocks that do perform well are expected to outperform the current market from here on out. Soon, you will see them getting more attention from the mainstream media, which pushes that herd mentality. Plus, buyers of call options are willing to pay these higher premiums for stocks in sectors that are super popular at the moment, which means that as the seller you'll get a higher return option without the risk.

General Motors, for example, was highly undervalued, and then the stock took a lot of time before it increased in the share price. People didn't believe that GM was even growing, and it was evident that people didn't really know whether or not they should invest. But, it had a strong trading pattern of about 36-40 for a long time, which means that it allowed for a lot of call writing, and eventually it increased by about 15-20% but is still a good company.

You also want to make sure that you have the volatility not super high. However if it does go high, expect it to increase, and it can lead to decreases in the value of the option, which means more money.

Best Buy might seem like a strange one to consider as a covered call option, because after all, with the era of Amazon taking over everything, you may wonder why in the world you should even consider this? Well, that's because it now has a steady stream of results and have made major changes to fight off the Amazon growth. Even though it did bottom out at $30 back in 2016, it actually doubled the share price over 2 years, so it's here to stick around.

They've been able to contain the sales issues that Amazon has done in the past, and even after the big recovery, it's still priced at just 12 times the forward earnings. While it isn't going to double again within the next 3 years, it does outperform the overall stock market, and the company now has more than double cash as total debt. It can buy back its own stock, and it does surprise wall street in the quarterly results, so it's a stock that, while it may not seem obvious, is a good one to consider.

You may wonder why the companies that are listed, such as USPS and the electric company are ideas. Well, with USPS, the downturn in prices of oil has helped with this. Fuel is one of the largest input places for UPS, and it wasn't fully factored into the guidance. UPS does announce the dividend increases, and it can increase to up to $1.00 for each share or more than that. UPS also has good buyback, and it has a buyback of almost 7%.

All of these are good options, but you should look for companies that have really good dividends that you know are going to increase. This will, in turn, generate money for you, even if you aren't going to be selling it anytime soon.

There are a few different factors that you can look at before you do find the right stock, and here, we'll give you a stock list criteria that you should always look at before you choose to invest:

• Make sure the stocks pay a dividend

• Make sure that it's reasonably valued at less than 15x the P/E ratio and less than 10x on the EV/EBITDA

• Make sure that the business model and how they make money is understandable to you

• Follow the trends for a few weeks to get a feel for trades

• Look at the valuation of the stock in the volatility that is placed there. You want to sell the high volatility, so make sure that they have that in the options

Follow this, and you'll have a good feel for your stock and the pricing.

How to Find the right Strike Price for A Covered Call

Finally, look at how you can look at the strike price for a covered call. As you start to work on this, you may wonder if you should have the strike price that goes with the options side. Covered calls do entail buying stock shares and selling them against there. The money, often called in this case the premium, that you get from this is in your account, but it is possible to set it up so that the price will increase. You should determine this by first looking at the option chain and using the quote system and look at the chain link. Narrow down your search to the options that are within 2-5 months into the future.

Make a note of the current share for this, and the strike price below the current stock, one that's close to it, and one that's above. So let's say the current price is 35.85, and you look at one with a $34 strike price quoted at $3.80 premium, and the $36 is $2.75, and the $38 is valued at $1.90

Put this all into a covered call calculator, one that you can find online, and from there, just input the numbers. Take the numbers, and from there, analyze the results, and compare the expected return if it remains unchanged and if it's called away. Look at the results for each one if they do end up staying unchanged, and you should then choose the strike price that you do think will go between now and the expiration date. The lowest price doesn't make much sense unless you think that it's going to definitely decrease with time. The other two are more fitting, but you should look and be realistic on how much of a growth this will get.

You should pick a strike price that is above the current share price, providing the potential for gains. Covered call calculators are good, and usually, they are good for the time period until it expires. You should pick strike prices in a more in-the-money option, especially if you want more downside protection with the option that the sock might be taken away. Out-of-the-money call options may result in your stock not being called, so you can sell more options in the same shares once the others expire. You always have to make sure that you multiply everything by 100 when working with it. So if it says $3.25, know that it's $325.

Covered calls are a wonderful way to make passive income, and you should take the time to best understand all of these so that you can create the best nest egg that you can, and the best profits possible.

A Short message from the Author:

Hey, are you enjoying the book? I'd love to hear your thoughts!

Many readers do not know how hard reviews are to come by, and how much they help an author.
I would be incredibly thankful if you could take just 60 seconds to write a brief review on Amazon, even if it's just a few sentences!
Please head to the product page, and leave a review as shown below.

Thank you for taking the time to share your thoughts!

Your review will genuinely make a difference for me and help gain exposure for my work.

A Step-By-Step Way to Sell Covered calls

Now that you know about how important it is to sell covered calls, and how they can help you, let's take a moment to go through the different options and how you can sell covered calls effectively. Here, we'll take you through each of the steps, and why they matter.

Step One: Beginning with Choosing the Underlying Security

The first thing that you need to make sure that you have is, of course, the underlying security, which is what you're going to sell to investors in order to have them try to purchase for lower, or higher than what it is on the market. The call option essentially allows for the person to potentially buy it in the future. The seller would be the one with the options that don't get rid of them until the person decides to buy the stock.

First, you need to choose security that works for you. Look at the different stocks that you own and look to see the ones that have good dividends, that you're willing to keep for a while, but if you did sell them, there wouldn't be much love lost. You should, for example, choose 100 shares of a stock that you own, and you can see that the stock is getting close to the price that you'd sell it. One option does equal 100 shares, so you'd write a single covered call on the stock that you have. Of course, not all stocks have underlying options, and usually, the stocks with underlying options are ones with a higher value.

Step Two: Calculating Before Writing

Before you execute this trade, you should make sure that you always make sure that you do look at how much you're going to get from this. If you feel like this covered call should be done at a certain time period, you should wait.

When you're back here, you'll want to put into the covered call calculator the stock price, options price, and the number of shares, and you may need to add in commission fees and margins, and you should make sure that you choose for the options excised to be there, and you can calculate. You should also choose whether the option exercised is set to **no** to see the difference. You can also look to buy-write or overwrite the stock that you have, and the broker can also add some instructions onto these too. Do put your covered call through the calculator before you begin.

While the sheet is relatively easy to fill out on your brokerage site, this prevents a lot of issues from coming about, and can also give you a good idea of what you're going to do next.

Step Three: Heading to the Brokerage to Fill Out the Sheet

Next, you got to your brokerage and go to the options order entry form, which is where you look at the contract you're putting together, the limit price, the stop price, the transaction, order type, duration, and also the expiration date.

Next, remember that options expire every third Friday, so you should always make sure that you do this. Now, you should look at the stock itself, see what the strike price for this, and what you're willing to sell for, and the premium price on this. Let's say that if it does close higher, it will get exercised, so you lose the stock, but the thing is, you're still making money. But if it's lower, you get to keep the shares, and the premium, which means that it's literally just posting, having people purchase options, and then rinse and repeat.

Remember that one contract equals 100 shares of stock, so if you have 300 shares of stock, only do one at a time. The limit price and order type are also important to make sure that you have a limit there to prevent them from selling or falling to a different price.

There is also the transactions tab, which is where investors get confused. **This is usually the "sell to open" option, which means that you're selling this to open the position. If you want to buy back the one that you sold, or buy long, you choose the option of buy to close.**

You can then choose the duration, and how long it will stay, and you can also choose all-or-none with this, and you choose whether or not you can trade this. You can't usually choose the preferred ECN but leave it on auto.

Step Four: Watching the Market

At this point, you've got three options for well, your option and covered call, and they're important to note. The first is the stock goes down, so the call will be worthless, and you have to sell it for the price of the option. If you notice that it takes a dive before the expiration date, don't freak out. While there might be some losses, you'll notice that the stock itself goes down in value, so you can buy it back for less money than you got to sell it. If the option on the stock is changed, you close the position, buy back the call contract, and go from there.

So let's say that you have an options contract that's going for $100 and the strike price is $105. If the price goes all the way down to 20, you might have to sell the stock at that price if someone bought a contract for it, but if you still have the premium, you can then buy it again for that low price. You will have to sell if the option is exercised, but again, this is something that you can decide for yourself, and if someone buys a contract.

There is also the option that it stays the same or goes up but doesn't reach too high. This isn't that bad, because the call option will expire, so you pocket the premium, and you will still have the stock that you initially had. Not something that you can complain about.

Finally, you have scenario 3, and that is that the stock rises above what the strike price is. If this happens, then you're going to assign the call option to this stock, and that means you will be forced to share those 100 shares of stock. So, unfortunately, you still lose the stock. Most of the time though, since you're still netting a profit, there isn't as much love lost as you might think.

But, there is another issue that comes about with this. That is, if the stock skyrockets after you sell the shares, you're probably going to notice that you could've netted a huge profit from this. This is when a lot of investors tend to kick themselves for this, but the truth is, you shouldn't do that. This is actually a decision that you made when you chose to part with the stock at the strike price that you desired, and you still achieved profit from this.

That is the common problem a lot of investors face when it comes to selling stocks. They think that they shouldn't have done it just because the price for it skyrocketed to a whole different height. But, that's not always the case. You shouldn't feel down about this, and it can be a bit disheartening, but realize that you're not terrible for choosing the option to part with this. Sometimes, you may not even realize that the stock is going to fluctuate with time, and that is why, when you're choosing stocks for covered calls, they should be stocks that would very rarely have that much of a rise in price, and while having that volatility is good, you should also make sure that it isn't so volatile that you can't predict how it may go next.

When it comes to improving your covered calls, the best thing to do is to research and hold onto the stock. If you do have older stock that you just don't want to hold onto anymore, then I do suggest that you consider the option of writing covered calls on them. Remember, there are always times when you can buy these back too, so if you want to get the stock back and cash in on those dividends, it can be quite worth your while to do this.

Writing Tips

At this point, there are a few tips that you can utilize before you submit the first covered call, and here, we'll highlight what those are.

You will want to pick a stock that's performed well each time, and you can always check to see if the call option is possible here. If you have old stock that people don't really care for anymore, you're pretty much screwed. You should avoid choosing stocks that are bullish for the long term because if you do end up losing it, you won't have to feel as bad because there is a chance that if the market is bull in that regard, you could lose your stock.

Next, you want to always factor in the strike price, and you should make sure that it's out of the money than in the money.

When you first start, you should choose a good expiration date that's easy for you to manage, and you should choose one that provides an acceptable premium for the call option and the strike price.

Usually, you want to have it around 2% of the stock to look for. Remember that time is money with this, and the future you go out of the contract, the more the option will be worth. However, the further you go into the future, the harder it can be to predict.

You should make sure that if the premium is high, there's a reason for it. If you notice that it isn't really good to invest in, you should probably opt out of this.

There are many investors that use covered calls as a foray when it comes to options trading. There is a risk, of course, but the actual risk comes from the stock itself, not from the sale of the call. The sale of this just limits only the opportunity on the flip side of this. When you are running a covered call, you should realize you're taking advantage of the time decay on your options sold.

Every day the stock doesn't move, and your call will decline in value and that, in turn, will benefit you as a seller. You should start to become familiar with time decay, and you should look to make sure that you see it in action. As long as the stock price never reaches the strike price, it won't get called away. Remember that. here's what's cool about this too: if you wanted to grab say, five stocks, and you decided to do this with each stock at hand, you're going to make a serious chunk of money. With every covered call that you do run, you'll become even more versed in the ins and outs of the market of options trading. So, it certainly can help you if you're wondering about how to take advantage of this. But, you should make sure that in the event, you do make mistakes, you learn about these and learn from them since they could end up costing you a pretty penny.

All About Buying Covered Calls

So we talked about selling a lot these last couple of chapters, and you may wonder if buying these covered calls is ever worth it, if in the event it is either below the price of the stock or right near it. The answer is yes, there are some serious benefits to be had when you buy covered calls, but it's a little different than selling these bad boys, so here, we'll go into deeper detail about buying covered calls, and why it may be beneficial to you.

What is Buying a Covered Call

Buying a covered call means that you're buying a stock at a certain price. For example, let's say that you are looking to buy some IBM stock. Instead of writing to get it at a certain price, you are buying it from the trader at a certain price, when the stock falls below a certain level.

So let's say the IBM stock is trading at $45 currently. You buy a covered call that says the stock will be sold at $40 a share. So, the stock goes up to $47, and you get that stock for $40, and essentially, you're saving $700 on the stock price. If it goes down to $39 somehow, you can't exercise this, and then, you end up losing out on the premium, whatever that may be.

The benefits of Buying Covered Calls

There are a few major benefits of buying covered calls, and here, we'll discuss how these purchases can benefit you.

First and foremost, if you're an investor looking to have more stock under your belt, you will want to buy covered calls. While you will have to pay a fee for those options, here is the thing: if the stock is predicted to drop super low, you can nab this up. At this point, you can have it under your belt for a fraction of what it might be otherwise.

Selling stock usually is a bit pricier than the covered call option, and if you're looking for options to nab this stock, then this is something you should consider.

What many don't realize, is that while yes, the investor can make some serious bank selling these, buying these from right under their noses has benefits too. When you buy them, you own them, which means you can do whatever you want with them.

So, that brings us to the second point. One way to invest in a smart manner is to buy the stock for cheap, and then turn around and then sell covered calls to this for a higher price. That way, you get the options fee from the next person, and you also can cash in on this.

That is the third benefit of this. You can cash in on this stock at any time too. So, let's say that the stock falls, you buy it for the covered call price, let's say the covered call price is .37 per share, so 370 dollars. If you then see the stock price immediately go up to say .50 a share, so

500 if you sell it, there you go, you made a 130-dollar profit. You also can cash in on the dividends of your stocks too.

There is also another benefit to buying covered calls: the type of stock you're getting. These stocks aren't just sitting in limbo not doing a darn thing. Instead, they are fluctuating a lot, and this will, in turn, mean that you can potentially cash in on this, or even sell more covered calls based on what you're doing. You will realize over time that the stock you get with this is actually very volatile compared to others, or it has a lot of impact on our economy somehow. These are also industries that won't be leaving anytime soon, such as energy industries.

Buying covered calls also adds to your portfolio. If you want to be taken seriously as an investor, I do suggest that you start adding to your portfolio. This will, in turn, showcase to other investors, and even your broker, your potential. You also can sell these at any time, net the cash, put it in the options account, and it could help you potentially get to level 5 on investment.

So yes, buying is a great way to essentially set yourself up for success. While you have heard a lot about how selling essentially puts you in control and generates a great retirement, you can really take advantage of buying too when it comes to options trading. Covered calls are bought for a reason, and while you may not see the advantages now, there are quite a few advantages that are ready to be exercised.

All About Open Interest

Let's talk about open interest. This is the total number of outstanding contracts, in this case, options, that haven't been settled for the asset. This doesn't count every buy and sell contract, but instead, this is a picture of the trading activity on the option, and whether the money is flowing about, and if the underlying stock is increasing, or decreasing under it all.

So what does that mean? Well, open interest is one of the data fields that you see when you look at the option, and that also includes the bid price, ask price, the implied volatility, and the volume too. Many traders ignore this, and this is actually a really bad thing to ignore.

Why is that? Well, essentially it doesn't update during the trading day, and you may not realize it, but sometimes this causes contracts to be exercised without you knowing it.

Let us use an example. You have 1000 shares of stock ABC, and you want to do a covered call, selling 10 of these calls, and you essentially would enter this into open. It is an open transaction and add 10 of these shares to the open interest. You're essentially entering the transaction to buy from closed, and that would decrease the open interest of this by 10 as well.

So let's say you are buying 10 of the ABC calls to open, and the other will buy 10 calls to close, the same number, so it won't change.

But why does this matter? Well, if you're looking at the total open interest, you won't know immediately whether the options are sold or bought, and this is why many ignore this. But, the truth is, this also has important information, and you shouldn't assume there is nothing there. One way to use this is to look at the volume of the contracts that you trade. When this starts to exceed the existing open interest, it does suggest that trading in that option is super high, which means lots are acting on it. You should potentially act on this if you feel that you're going to get a profit from acquiring that underlying stock.

Open interest also shows you the liquidity of this option as well. If there isn't an open interest for this option, there's no secondary market for the option itself. When options have a lot of open interest, it means that there are a lot of buyers and sellers out there. Active secondary markets then increase the odds of getting the option orders filled at relatively decent prices.

So if you have a more open interest, you're going to be able to trade this option at a reasonable spread between the ask and the bid.

Let us take another example. You see the open interest on a stock, such as maybe IBM, is 12,000. This does suggest that the market in this is active, and there might be investors that want to trade at this point. You see the bid price is just $1, and the option is $1.06, which means you can buy one call option contract at the price that is mid-market.

But, let's say that the open interest is like 3. This is practically no activity on those call options, and there isn't a secondary market because people aren't interested, so you will struggle to enter and exit this at a reasonable price.

Let us take maybe looking at say GameStop for example. After their recent reports, their stock is probably at an incredibly low open interest. That means you shouldn't try to act on that. But, Apple is currently putting out more products and is getting ready to shell out more flagship products, so their stock has a huge open interest on it, and that means, you should potentially consider entering and exiting it, and possibly buying covered calls on that stock for a good price.

Open interest doesn't get updated as much, but it is still of an important case to understand, and it can affect you rush in and approach a trade. It gives you a good indication of the overall trading volume on the stock; which makes it very significant.

The Risks of Covered Calls

With buying covered calls, you essentially are betting that the stock will go high enough that you can get it at the price you're trying to get it for. That is your number one risk.

But, how is that a risk? Well, whenever you're buying a call, you have to pay the person who is putting out the covered call a fee. Now, this fee may be a little bit; it may be a few hundred dollars.

In essence, you're betting that the stock will go up high enough that you can get that stock from them.

Now, let's take, for example, you see the stock currently at 100. Let's say the covered call is for 105, and you decide you want to get an options contract for that. So, you choose that, the time that elapses happens, but the stock never reaches 105, and it stays at 103. Well, unfortunately, you just lost out on some cash there because of that, because you were betting on t to go up so you could get a deal, and unfortunately, that didn't happen.

The thing with buying covered calls, is you need to make sure that you're getting stock that is going to increase within that timeframe, is at a price that you're willing to pay, and has a chance of potentially netting you a profit. If it does have all three of these then get into it and take that risk. But, what can be worrisome is how much you can potentially lose.

For example, let's say that you are interested in getting a stock that has the potential for growth. You decide to purchase some of the stock from investor X. Investor X has a covered call written out where you'll pay .95 per share, so after 100 shares, it's 950 dollars. You decide you go for it, and you get that 300-dollar fee paid to him. Swell, right?

Well, unfortunately, that stock does not increase. It doesn't decrease either, it just stagnates. You thought you had a chance to do this, but then, it ends up potentially doing nothing to help you. Lo and behold, you just lost that 300 dollars, the investor gets to keep that, and their shares too.

If you do that five times, with five different stocks, that's $1500 right there down the drain.

So remember that when you're looking into covered calls because this can potentially wreck you if you aren't careful.

Finding the Right Stock and Strike Price for a Covered Call

So how do you find the right stock for this? Well, again you want to find a stock that is going to have enough volatility where it will get to the price that you want it to be, pays decent dividends, and also is a field that will actually be around for a while.

One that currently is thriving is DSL actually. You may think that it isn't going to do as well, but it still holds an impressive number of dividends. That means if you can find stocks that are being sold, that have the potential to possibly change the game for the better later on, and also are worth investing in, you should do that.

You should look for a stock that you have a feeling you can easily get too. If there are a lot of open interests on the stock, I do suggest possibly taking your time and putting effort into that. You'd be amazed at the difference it can make.

You should also look at the different healthcare industries and service industries. What people don't realize, is that healthcare investors actually have a lot of good value to them. Shares for that can actually be quite high too, which means you can get instant payouts with a lot of these.

Options traders that buy calls also should be looking at the way the strike price is. You want a call that's right near a price of the stock, but a little bit higher. It actually should be something that is almost incremental, and you want to look at a stock that has enough volatility that it's actually moving about, but you have a chance to make some serious cash.

The goal for options traders that buy is they are buying a stock, hoping to get a 100% gain in a month. So you want that stock that you know, super fast, is going to net you some serious value.

While those stocks that are chugging about might seem like a good idea if your goal is to purchase and then net the dividends, though not every investor like this will want that end goal. What you want instead, is the ability to quickly turn around, net profits, and do so in short order.

You also want to look for calls that are quick, ones that don't have a lot of time value added to that. Why is that? Well, the longer you hold it, the lesser the value.

Whenever you buy call options, you're not only getting the share price higher to make money, and you need it to do so in a short timeframe. So that means you need to be watching the clock — options decay in value, which is bad for buyers. While the sellers love that, and they'll try to make an option continue on for time immemorial since they already got their cash, you need to work fast. You need to make sure that it's got a short expiration date but has the potential to hit that level. So you want something that is volatile, that has a life to it, and potential especially if you plan just to net those dividends of the stock itself, and overall is quick.

When it comes to the strike price, always try to shy towards the lower level of this. The lower it is, the better, because that will mean that you're going to get the right results from this, and ultimately can help you net a profit.

How to Buy a Successful Covered Call

So let's talk about how you buy a covered call and a stock that you want to have. How do you do it? Well, the answer is simple.

First, you must take a look at the stock that you want to buy, the shares, and what you're going to need to pay, especially against those premiums.

So, let's say you want to buy stock with Ford, because hey, Ford is releasing a new engine and car set, and you have a feeling it will increase in price. You can do this with Apple as well because there are rumors the MacBook Pro 2019 is coming out next month or something. Lots of people like to jump on the apple covered calls right before the reveals of their iPhones. So you log into your account, and from there look for the stock that has a price in the range that you want. You want the strike price to be a decent amount, such as maybe 14 dollars a share per 100 shares. Now, when you're inside, you choose the call that you want to buy, and maybe you choose that call option and look to see how many days this will go. You should from there, choose the option to get this call. Once you're going to do there, if you're going to right click, and choose what you want to do with the covered stock and choose that you want a contract for this one. You may be taken at this point to the page to fill out the information, and you should from there, look to see what your cost basis is going to be, and the amount that you're going to pay. You should look for a decent price on the shares, and make sure that you're not letting them fall too much.

If the stock is falling, do not take it. That's a sinking ship, and you can say goodbye to that. But, once you choose this, you then will start to look at the stock, and once you see that the shares are at a higher price than what you bought the covered call for, you can then log in, and choose to exercise this.

At this point, once you've exercised it, the investor will be obligated to sell you the option, and from there, you can now buy the covered call option that you want at the price that is listed.

Now, let's take the flip side. Suppose maybe you didn't see the trends changing all that much, and it became a stagnated stock. Unfortunately, the longer you hold out, the less fluctuation is going to happen on the stock. Your goal is to get out of there as fast as possible. The problem is, over time, that stock will stay at that range. You want to invest the moment you know there is a big change.

So yes, right before the Apple reveal will be great, the stock goes up, you cash in on that option immediately. But, let's say that it's been a slower month, and you end up not doing anything with it. Well, the investor you bought it from will get to collect it.

Now, if you invested in say, GameStop which is currently struggling, and then, you notice that even with the summer releases nothing happens, you're basically just paying someone a few hundred for a stock that's a sinking ship. Remember that and try to avoid the sinking ships as much as possible.

When you get the stock, however, you can always trade it again for a higher right, open up your own covered calls on it (with the risk of losing the stock of course) or just cash in on those dividends. Remember, once you get it, you do have the power to do what's best for you.

What About Naked Calls?

Another area we should touch on is naked calls, and this is a very risky type of trade that has some reward, but for the most part, shouldn't be attempted unless you've done trading of this nature before. Naked calls usually are taken when the investor thinks that the stock price will fall below the strike price when it expires. The max possible gain is the premium collected once the option is sold. It's achieved when the option is held and expires, rendering it worthless. The call allows the owners to purchase this at a predetermined price on or before the date of the expiration. If you're selling the call without the stock under it and is exercised by the buyer, you'll then be left with a short position on the stock.

When you write naked calls, the risk is actually unlimited, and this is where people get in trouble. Compared to puts, there is actually much more risk there for various reasons. Most options usually expire worthlessly, so the trader might have more winning trades than losing ones. This is what you want for a few good reasons, and the main factor at hand being the fact that if you do end up losing a trade, you do end up losing a bunch of gains.

To put it simply, one singular bad trade can wipe out an entire year's gains, or even so much more. You need to have sound money management, and always know the risk control when you trade in this fashion.

You need to have some risk controlling strategies on hand, and the easiest is to simply cover the position by either buying the offsetting option or even the underlying stock. If the underlying stock is grabbed, then the position isn't naked anymore, and it will incur the extra risk that's there. Some will incorporate risk control, but you need to basically know options trading beyond a basic understanding.

Usually, these are done months closer to the expiration dude to the fact that time decay is actually one of the best things about this type of trade, since the closer you get to expiration, the faster the time decay will erode the premium there. While this does have unlimited risk, if you choose the strike prices wisely, it will alter the risk of exposure as well. The further away this is from there, the current market is trading, the more the market will move in order to make this worth something during expiration.

Let's now look at an example of this. You make a hypothetical trade mentioned that a trader expects the stock to be lower for a few months or that the trend would have a sideways trade. Let's say that the shares are trading at $20 a share, and at the time of the trade, you have $22.50 calls trading at $1. A naked call writer would be established that by the way 22.50 naked calls wouldn't be sold, bringing in $100 per option sold, which essentially means that you're getting at least $100. Now, if this stock does sell below the 22.50 at the time of the expiration, the option is worthless, and you get to keep the premium for this. Sounds nice, right? Well, if it ends up going higher, this is where the trouble happens, and the option will be exercised, and you'll have to deliver the stock at $22.50 a share, which is $2250 dollars. Yikes!

But, let's say that you have the cost basis for the short X being about $21.50 a share, you risk the difference between whatever it's trading above $21.50. You can see that makes the max risk unknown, and while it may only be $2250 that you lose, if it ends up going higher, you could end up losing so much more. This is why money management and understanding the risk of it is so important and why people need to understand this before they go into it.

Because these naked calls are with unlimited risks, most brokerage firms require you to have a large amount of capital or worth in addition before you make these type of trades. You'll want to make sure that before you even think about trying anything risky, you talk with your brokerage of this. You should also become familiar with the margin requirements for these positions, which do vary. If you're trading at a firm that doesn't specialize in this; you may find the margin requirements not very reasonable.

This is an advanced form of trading however, and it's something that for the most part people aren't going to mess with, due to the fact that in many cases, they don't have the capital needed for this. Also because there is a chance that you don't want to take the risk of this either, because people have lost a good nest egg just from a botched naked call trade.

For many people, covered calls are a great way to invest in the stock, and if you're looking to buy them, make sure that you follow the directions to doing so, and make sure that you do fully understand what it is that you're doing.

Buying and Selling Puts

Next, let's talk about buying and selling puts. Puts, of course, allow you to sell the stock that you have or the underlying commodity that you have underneath it all. There are different reasons why people may want to buy or sell puts, and here we'll go over what it is, how to do it, and the advantages of such.

What is Buying and Selling Puts?

Selling/buying puts essentially is giving someone the option to buy the stock at a certain amount of money.

If you sell a put option, you're selling the chance for someone to buy that stock at a price.

If you buy a put option, you're giving someone the option to buy that stock for that price and the person is obligated to sell it.

So, let's say that you're planning on getting a put option to buy that stock at a certain amount of money. You can put that option down, and from there, wait for it to fall, and from there you can exercise it. Maybe you want to buy shares from a really good railroad company. You essentially notice it's increasing the earnings on this, and you decide to potentially buy the stock when it's under 30. By buying a put option, it basically makes the seller obligated to sell you the stock when it falls below 30 dollars.

You want to exercise these in falling markets since you'll generate a profit when the market is falling, rather than rising.

Selling Puts in this Market

Here's the thing, when you want to sell puts, you should only do so if you're comfy with the owning stock that's under it at the price that's there because essentially, you're assuming the obligation to buy it if the person does decide to sell. From this, you should also only enter trades where the net price paid for the security is good. This is the most important part of selling puts profitably in the markets that you have. There are other reasons to sell it to the person. You also can own the security below the market price that is currently there, and you'll definitely want to be careful when you do choose to sell this.

An Example of Buying a Put

Let us now move onto buying these puts. One thing to note is that you're not going to see the commissions, taxes, margins, and other charges factored into any of these equations for a reason. That starts to get it a bit more complicated, and right now, we are just showing you the cut and dry of all of the ways you can buy a put option that can be considered. But, you should definitely consult with your tax advisor or broker before you go in.

So the simplest way to bet against stocks is to get put options. Put options essentially give you that right to sell it at a certain price by a time period. You essentially pay the premium, which will from there will sell you that stock at that price.

So let's say you've got company A, which is overvalued currently at $50 bucks a share, and you decide to bet on a decline at this point, getting a put contract that's at $35 a share, and it costs $2 per share, so the "breakeven" price is $33 a share. This is deduced from basic math, since you're taking the contract price of 35 minus the 2 making it $33 for this. Since each of these represents 100 different shares. That's $3500 in total of what you'll buy, and then of course it'll cost you upfront $200 for this (cause of the options contract and the shares) and from there, you enter the trade.

Now, let's say that the option contract is for August 2019, and from there, you fast-forward and watch the market. Below is a table of what can happen

Action of stock	What happens to you	Your return	Outlook
Soars all the way up to $60	The option expires, becomes worthless, and you lose the $200 premium, but you're basically losing nothing else	(100%)	Okay
Falls slightly to $38	Same thing happens, stock falls but you don't make a profit	(100%)	Okay
Drops all the way to $25	You make some cash! 800 dollars to be exact ($35-25) and then the $2 premium	(800%)	Nice!
Drops to $0 (basically going bankrupt)	The ideal situation, and you'll get $3300 from it (0 at expiration, so 3500-200 from the premium)	(1500%)	Ideal!

So the best time to use these is when you have a sinking ship in terms of stock. Otherwise, they aren't worth your time, and it's better to not have these stocks, and there is always a chance you could end up losing money. But, if the person sells the stock, and you turn around and cash in on it, you'll have more money, and you don't have to worry about the burden of a stock.

If you choose to buy it when it declines, you're essentially going to get money from this. You want to do it when it's declining and nothing more. It is very important that you don't choose to act on these types of options until it's that time.

That's it, that's all buying put options is, and you want to make sure that it falls to the level that you want it to be at.

The risks of it

Risks are still there in both cases. Options are risky due to the complex nature of this, but once you know how these work, it can reduce the risk a whole lot. Put options, in particular, can be quite risky, especially for the seller, since they may have to spend more money buying back the option that they once had.

One other aspect of this, especially for buyers is the break-even aspects of it. So, let's assume that you got a stock today for $46 and this was at $44, which is two points down what it is there, so you'll be profitable in the trade. But, here's the thing, you're going end up losing out on money due to the fee for the option. It would make the option worth $2 since you spent $4 on it, so that means you're losing out on it.

But there is also the fact that if the option does expire and you're in-the-money, you'll get the right stock immediately. You may not realize it, but these can be quite good, especially for plunging markets, especially if you know they will bounce back.

If you end up seeing it go high, you're going to end up paying for that premium to get the right to buy it, and that's money that can rack up to a couple of thousand dollars. Do make sure that you understand that when you do choose to figure out your own stock, and how you can easily rectify.

The Advantages of Buying Puts

Buying puts, which gives you an option to sell the stock at a given price, is good if you're looking to protect yourself. So let's say that you have this stock, or you've been eyeing a stock that will probably fall, and then rise over the next few months. There are those out there, and usually, it's due to lulls in the market at the time. So, you decide to buy the put that's there, which gives you the option to sell that stock when the market decides to resurface at a higher level.

For you, you're taking a gamble on this, because the market may not recover, but if you notice a stock that could potentially have the power to possibly fall, this may be a good one. That way, you can get the stock for cheaper. From there, you can sell the stock again, and you have the right to sell that stock at the price that you're looking for.

It essentially allows you to form that extra security in his, which is a nice little advantage for the person who wants to sell it. Long puts are good for this, especially if you want to sell these.

Put options let you sell this asset at the strike price that's there. With this, the seller is then obligated to purchase these shares from the holder. Now, how can this help? Let's say that you buy a stock at 20 bucks, and then you compare it to 20 dollars at the edge that's there. If the price is below 20 at any point, you can actually then exercise the options and reduce the losses. This can definitely help, especially if you're willing to buy an option, and from there, sell it in order to avoid lots of trouble.

The Advantages of Selling Puts

So let's take the flip side of this. When you sell puts, this allows for the trader of this to sell the shares and the underlying stock at the price that's there in the contract, should the shares move below the strike price. This allows you to have some leverage, and often, long puts allow you to make money. It does give the buyer a little bit of leverage, but here's the thing, for sellers, you can then make money from this. Let's say that the strike price doesn't ever fall below that. You get to keep your premium, and the other person will lose out on money.

So, let's say that you have a stock, and the problem is that it's got high expectations, but a technical weakness, trading at about $45 a share, but the trader thinks that it will fall. The seller of this doesn't think it will fall at all. Let's say that you decide to open up an options contract for $55 then since that's where you believe it will stay, at $3.50 a share. Now, let's say that the stock doesn't actually finish below the breakeven point, which is the strike price minus the debit that's there. This is often determined by how the share will fail by the expiration date,. Now let's say that it doesn't fall at all. That means that you get to keep that money, and from there, you can sell.

But, for a seller, this can potentially mean you are losing your stock if it falls, and from there, it will then have the intrinsic value of the loss that's there, and for the most part, you can get big returns. From there, the seller could always buy the shares back at an amount, and while they can get a small profit, it only is returned by the risk at hand.

Meanwhile, let's say that the stock moves up to $55 in this. The person looking to buy will be out the money that they paid for the option, but on the other hand, the shares that you will have now will cost more to buy back, which is a loss.

So basically, you want to make sure that it will fall as a trader too, because you can potentially end up losing out on some serious cash if you're looking to sell puts. That is because if you sell it at that, and choose to buy it at that, you'll definitely create a lot of problems for yourself, and for your business.

When you sell puts, you have an obligation to buy the security at a price that's predetermined to the buyer that exercises the option. Buying means that you have the right to sell this at a price.

How to find the right Put for Yourself

When choosing put options to buy, traders need to understand the expectations for these stocks, including where this is going, and how long it will take to get to the next point. Once you answer all of these questions, you can from there look to find the right strike price that's there. If you see a stock that is falling and you have a chance to nab it for a good price, and then turn around and sell the shares, this might be good. You also don't want something with a super long expiry date, since that can end up biting you in the butt later on.

But, there are actually a couple of other factors that you will want to look into when you're looking to get into puts, especially on the buyer's side. This is the volatility of this. You want volatility that is either low or undervalued, meaning that it isn't changing all that much. You should look at the Schaeffer's Volatility Index in order to figure out if you're overpaying or underpaying for stock in terms of options. You can look at the implied volatility of the front-month options and the money that is there. From there, you should use a percentile rank, and determine if the option is cheap, or expensive, especially in terms of volatility. Stocks with the SVI near the bottom are actually pretty good for a short-term option, so make sure you understand that.

You want a stock that will fall and will fall long enough for you to get into it and sell what you have. You also want to look at a prolonged bear market cycle, which means that it's declining, and this is probably one of the best strategies for that type of market. You should definitely look to see if there is a chance that it will be able to be mitigated when you choose to sell this once the stock goes through as well.

You don't want to choose a company that's got like super high stock, because that's not how you're going to profit. You should, in turn, help you get the asset, and from there sell this. When you get a put option, you'll know how much you're going to lose when you do this. However, it also is good to understand that if you put it in there, you also will know how much you're going to make, versus the volatile pricing that selling it would normally produce.

You want to look for ones that decrease in value but will be long enough to get a profit off it, and you will want to look for assets that are making the 90-day price lows. This is actually a good thing because assets that do trade at this 90-day asset will move lower with time. You should make a list of some of the assets that you feel will have a good impact on what you're trying to achieve, and from there, you can also look at the criteria and the technical indicators that will be there during the main downtrend.

You always want to trade in the direction of the trend that's there when working with put options, so you should make sure that the asset is slowly moving lower with time. The biggest mistake that you can make is going against the main trend, and that's a huge mistake.

You want to wait then for the asset to reach a 90 day price low, or break below that, and from there, you wait for the pullback against that and the price low, and you can use technical indicators in order to figure out the pattern and look at the pullback, and the best time to buy put options. You should do this especially before the asset reverts itself in the trend, which is definitely something that happens almost every time, one for one, with trading.

You should also look for options that are in and out the money because these do factor into how much you're going to get out of this. You should look at the market price of the option at any time as well, and the odds of it expiring are in the money. The closer that it gets to in the money, the more it will be worth, and the further that is, the less it will be worth.

How close or how far you choose these options is determined by the price, the move you're expecting from your underlying asset. If you're expecting a smaller price move, for example, you would want an in-the-money option. But, if you're expecting it to just nosedive sharply over time, chances are you'll want them out of the money put option because it will provide more leverage in different circumstances. But remember, every single person's option can be different, and there is a lot that you will want to work with and take on when you're trying to put together different options. The right trading will allow for a much better, more worthwhile trading market, and in turn, it will help make everything so much more profitable with time.

The Rookie Mistake

The biggest mistake rookies can have, are they fail to take into account the factors of volatility. Just because you get the puts and the stock drops, that isn't how it works. If you buy a long put option, you want to capitalize on the volatility spikes, but this hurts you when you're buying puts. For example, during these earnings, this risk can elevate because of the uncertainty of it. But once the company announces this, it mitigates the risk, and at this point, market players will decide on the information for the company. You can utilize buying spreads in this, which we're going to touch on later. But, the best way to tell if the options are expensive or not is to look at the previous trends. Do take some time to look into that, and why they matter.

Why Puts are the Solution for Option Prices Plunging

The market is always volatile, and you need to understand that buying puts is actually a really good way to help minimize the losses in a market that is declining. If you go into long puts, you will want to focus on the speculation of the falling share prices. The main difference between this and married puts, which we will talk about later on to help you and your portfolio if you get into a pickle, is that there is no ownership in the shares that are under this. The only ownership is in the puts. Opening this position is definitely good because you can buy the position, or close this. Closing a position means that you're buying back what you were selling later.

Besides buying, you should look as well as how you can profit from the falling share prices that the stock that's shelling short. You can do this by borrowing shares, and from there selling them. Once the price falls, you buy them back at a lower price.

This is one of the main reasons why people will buy and sell puts. Buying puts instead of just shorting these are great, and it is one of the main reasons why people will do this. It is why people buy calls too, and why some people find this advantageous as well. It allows you to have leverage, which allows you to put stocks that you can't find the shares to be short. Yes, there are some stocks that you may not be able to short, but this gives you the option to do so. Some stocks found on Nasdaq can't be shorted due to the fact that brokers don't have enough shares to lend to the people that would like to short these. It can become useful since this can be a profit from the "non-sharable" stock. It also puts you at inherently less risk than shorting the stock, because the most you end up losing is the premium that you paid for the put itself, so much less in terms of the potential that you can lose.

Closing out the position usually involves selling or exercising, and you should look at this whenever you notice that there is a chance that you can make a profit. If you do wish to exercise the put, you will then put, or then sell the shares for the amount that you have, because you have a contract, and you can net a profit. The distinction between these is important to understand, and understanding what you're getting into is very important, and you need to understand that these puts can be volatile. You should understand the payoff that you're getting from this and the max value that you're potentially going to make from this.

At the bottom of this, puts are a great way to get profits when the stock is falling, but I don't suggest getting into these until that happens. This does have a lot of advantages over shorting a stock, and it can potentially net you a profit if you know that the stock is on the decline, but you need to be careful with this, and not over-leverage the positions that are there. When you use this properly, you can profit from the downsides, and make sure that your losses aren't limited. They are good, but I do suggest not getting super into these just yet, because they can be quite frustrating for the newbie beginner, and I do suggest getting with your broker before you begin with this. That way, you can get a feel for what it is that you need to do as well.

Naked Puts

There are also naked puts, which is an advanced put options strategy, so I don't suggest trying this till you've worked with basic puts. The reason for that is because of they're incredibly risky.

What does it mean to trade an option naked though? It doesn't mean that you're going to the stock exchange in the buff, but rather, you're selling the options without having a position in the underlying instrument. For example, if you're writing a naked put, you're selling a put without having the stock. If you do have the stock underneath it, it's actually covered. Hence, why we call them covered calls and such because the stock is underneath there.

The concept is for only advanced traders because it does involve a lot of profit potential. Yes, but also a risk, and you need to have money management as well. You should understand the riskiness of this, and don't do it until you've got some experience underneath your belt.

So naked put means where you put a put option underneath there, without any stock. The risk exposure is essentially the main difference between this and a naked call.

Naked puts are used when the investor expects the stock to be above the strike price at the time of the expiration. Similar to naked calls, the potential for print is limited to the premium that you have. A person can make the most of the stock if it's traded above the strike price at the expiration, and it expires and becomes worthless. If this happens, you're keeping the entire premium.

While this has unlimited risk in some ways, that's actually not the case. The risk of the naked put is different from the call, in that the trader could lose most if the stock goes all the way to zero. There is still significant risk there when compared to the reward you get, and unlike the naked call, if this does get exercised against you, you'll get the receiving stock. This is opposed to getting a short position on the stock, as in the case of the naked call, and you can hold the stock as part of the possible exit strategies as well.

So what is the risk? Well, there is the risk that you could end up having to pay for all of the stock, and if it plummets, you're going to end up being stuck with a dying ship, that's for sure.

As an example, let's take stock X, and let's say that you see it trade on March 1st at about $45 a share. So, for the sake of simplicity, and let's assume that the may 44 puts are over there at $1. If we sell that, we'll get a $100 for every single put that's sold. If it trades above the $44 share at expiration, it will then be worthless, and we'll get $100 for every single option sold.

But, let's say that it falls below the price of that when it expires. Well, we can from there except for the Y to be assigned to our stock, with 100 shares of that, at the price of $44, so it will cost about $4400 for everything. If you're looking to potentially have the cost basis at say $43, a share, you'll immediately see the losses there.

However, contrary to naked call, you'll see the max loss on this being $4300 on this, and it would only be if the stock went to zero, which is unlikely in the index , but possible if you have individual stock.

Usually, these requirements for this are a little more accommodating, and that's because if the put is exercised and you get the stock, as opposed to short stacking, as in the naked call, the maximum risk exposure is the value of the stock position and is less than what the premium received for the put option is.

This is a risky process, and it may seem like easy money, but that's far from the case. It's an exact science, so remember that next time you consider doing this type of trade.

Puts are a good way to get some different investments, just make sure that you know what you're doing, and you understand the market before you try most of this.

Advanced Strategies

Now let's talk advanced, shall we? Let's take a moment to talk about these, and while they are much more advanced than what they usually require from a person beginning with options trading, they should be known. People will want to consider these if they're thinking of trying to make it in the game. Here, we'll talk about some of the advanced strategies that are important to understand.

Buying Straddles

Straddles, otherwise known as a long straddle, is a strategy that works in a neutral market, and it involves buying a put, and a call at the same time of the same underlying stock, price, and the expiration date. This is a strategy that allows for unlimited profit, limited risk options in their strategies, and these are used especially when the trader thinks that the securities under this will experience a lot of volatility in this.

Now, this allows the investor to benefit from a significant move in the stock price, whether it goes up or down, and the approach consists of getting equal amounts of a call and put options with the expiration date. The straddle focuses on a common strike price.

Options are usually a type of security, so the price of this is linked to the price of something else. When you buy options, you get the right, but not the obligation, to sell or buy the asset under it at a set price on or before a date beforehand. A call option gives the investor the right to get stuck and put gives you the right to sell the stock. The stock must rise above for calls or below for puts so that the position is exercised for the profit.

Straddle trade works with a price movement that has a lot of volatility. Let's say there's a company that's working on releasing the latest earnings results in the three-week duration, but you don't know if the news is good or bad. The weeks beforehand would be a good time to add a straddle, since when the report is released, the stock will move sharply higher or lower. So, you want to buy it at a common price.

Let's say that it's trading $15 in April, and then, you have a $15 for the month of June, and it's got a put price of $2, but the price of a $15 call is $1. A straddle is achieved by getting both the call and the put, both of which are 100 and 200 dollars respectively. You'll then have $300 in premium to pay on this. It will increase the straddle if the volume of the stock moves higher, because of the long call, or if the stock goes lower. There is a long call and a long put placed on both of these, and the profits will be realized as long as the price of this moves by at least $3 in each direction. If you know that it's going to be like that, do go for this, but if you don't think the volatility will be more than $3, then this isn't wise for you to do.

You essentially calculate the maximum profit, which is unlimited, and you look at the profit achieved when the price of the underlying is three, and the strike price of the long call and the net premium or price of the underlying, which is lower than the strike price of the long put and the premium paid.

If you get a profit, you're essentially looking at the strike price minus the net premium paid or the strike price of the long put, and the price of the underlying, and the net premium paid on this.

Maximum loss for these long straddles happens when the stock price on the expiration date is trading at the strike price for the options that are bought. At this price, it's essentially totally worthless, and both won't benefit the trader, and the trader will lose the entire initial debit.

There is also the breakeven point, with the upper being the strike price plus the net premium, and the lower is the price of the put, minus the net premium paid.

So, suppose you've got a stock trading at $40 in June, and you decide to have a long straddle there with a Jul40 put and call each for 200 dollars, which is your max profit loss. The biggest amount you'll lose is essentially the option price.

So, if the stock is then trading at $50, it will then make the call in the money, and it has an intrinsic value of $1000 in terms of increase. Essentially, you're pocketing $600 from that trade.

But, let's take it on another level, let's say that you end up seeing them both at $40 at the end of this, and you lose the total profit of what you have. So you're losing $400, which kind of stinks, but it's not the worst.

Essentially, you are possibly going to end up getting a loss and losing only what you paid for the option at most, and you should definitely consider looking at the brokerage commissions as well. It does vary in amount, but they are great for making sure that you have the right volatility strategies in place.

You can also use short straddles, and they are used when you know that little movement is expected at the stock price, again benefitting you.

Buying Strangle

This is the other option when looking to buy based on tends. While straddles don't really have much of a directional basis, the strangle is used when you believe that the stock has a much higher chance of going in a certain direction, but also protect you if you think there will be a negative move.

So, let's say you believe a company will have results that are positive, which means you don't need as much downside protection, instead of buying the put option with the strike price of say $15 for $1, you buy the put maybe at $12.50 with a price of $0.25, which isn't as much. The trade would cost a lot less than the straddle and requires less of a move to break even. The lower strike put option in this protects you against the extreme downside, putting you in a better position and chance to gain from the positive announcement.

It is often called the long strangle, and this one is much more of a neutral strategy than others in trading, and often it does involve sometimes getting an out-of-the-money put, or a call on the same stock and the expiration date being the same too. This allows for unlimited profit again, and limited risk in this, and it's good for options traders that think it will have volatility in the singular direction, rather than both directions. Usually, long strategies are debit spreads, and a net debit is taken in this trade.

This one involves a lot of movement in one way or another direction. For the most part, the max profit is achieved, and you get profit when the price of the underlying and the strike price of the call and the net premium is less than the price of the long put or the net premium paid.

The maximum loss in long strangle is usually when the stock price in expiration is between the strike prices of the options that you get. At that point, both options are worthless, and the options trader loses the initial debit that was taken to enter the trade, so you basically lose the premium. You essentially lose the most based on your premium, and the commissions paid. Usually, the breakeven points are based on the strike price of both of these, and the premium paid, so that's where most of the losses come from.

For example, let's say you've got another stock, also trading at $40 in June. The options trader decides to get a JUL 35 put, and a JUL 45 call for $100 on each of those, so they're $200 in commissions total, which is also the max profit loss. So, let's say that the stock immediately trades at $50 in expiration, which puts the 35 as worthless, but the 45 call is worth it, and since that has a value of $500, you essentially make a $300 profit, since $500 is what you make, minus the premium that you need to pay for all of those, which was $200.

On the flip side, let's say that you notice the company's profit immediately go down to $25, and that gives you a profit margin of $1000, and while the 45 call is worthless, you're going to still get some results from the 35 put, which in turn means that you end up profiting about $800, again because you take the intrinsic value minus the premium.

With these, you need to also take your commissions into account, and while they're small, they're also fees that you will need to pay in order to put that trade in there.

You can also do these short if you want it to spread a little bit when you notice that there won't be much movement in the underlying stock price.

Options strangles are similar to straddles, but this one is good because it saves you as an investor both money and time in trading, especially if you're on a tighter budget.

You may wonder if you should use a long strange or a short strangle. Well, if you are looking to see if there is movement in the longer term, and you think that after a while it will have this change, you can create a "long strangle" position. On the flip side, if you think you're going to only see one quick fluctuation before it's back in the same position it was before, it will then be known as a short strangle. However, no matter what type of strangle you use, the success or failure of this is based on the limitations that you can get, and the supply and demand of it.

There are some factors that affect both strangles and straddles, and here, we'll dive into these three factors to know for both.

The first is the out-of-the-money options. This can be executed using these types of options, and they can be up to half the expense of what the in-the-money options are. It also depends on the capital that you're working with. If a trader puts a long strangle on something, you can trade both at 50% on this, and it can be much less than what the potential loss that you could potentially set yourself up for otherwise.

The other factor is the risk/reward and the limit of volatility. This is a second difference between the straddle and the strangle is that the market might not move at all. The strangle involves the sale of options that may be OTM, and from there, there's a risk of exposure to the risk that there might not be enough change in the asset under this in order to make the market move outside the resistance and support range. For traders that are long in strangles, this might be the worst thing that can happen, but the limited volatility is what can be used to profit from this.

The final factor that plays into positions is delta, which is known as the volatility of this, and it can affect your decisions, in order to show how closely the value of the option changes in ratio to the underlying asset that's there. An OTM option can move up to 30% on some cases, but the best way to determine whether this will benefit you is you should look at the delta of the purchases you're thinking of selling. If you're in a long strangle, you want to make sure that you're getting the maximum move-in option value for what you're paying for. If you're shorting it, you'll want to make sure that this is likely to expire, with low delta, and offset the unlimited risk that should be there as well. Look into each of these and determine for yourself whether or not you're in a position that can be affected by this or not.

If you're dead certain a stock will make a move, you should consider getting a long straddle than a strangle. While a straddle may cost more, the stock won't make such a big move to reach one of the break-even points, so remember that.

The Call Ratio Backspread

This is another options strategy that is a much more advanced form of options trading, but some users may use it if they think that the underlying stock or the security will rise by a lot. Essentially, this combines the sales and purchases of an option in order to see the limited loss potential and the mixed profit potential. However, the gains can be significant if the underlying financial instrument starts to rally.

So how is this done? Well, it's essentially created by selling, otherwise known as writing, a call option, and from there, using the collected premium in order to purchase a greater number of call options that have the same expiration, but a higher strike price. This one has potentially unlimited profit on the upside, since the person trading has more options that are long call rather than short options.

Now remember that call options give the person the right to buy a stock at a certain price, but they aren't obligated to do it, and they must do so within a specific time period. So remember that if you get a call option with say, the strike price being about $10, you'll see that the stock is trading at $10, it trades at the money. If you notice the stock rises, your option will make money, and if it falls, it will then make the investor only lose the premium, but they will also never own the stock as well.

So why does this matter to the call ratio backspread? Well, essentially this backspread allows for the investor to purchase these call options on a stock that's out of the money, which means that the strike price is higher than the stock price. So, let's say that a stock is currently trading at $15 at the moment currently on the market. You may buy the options at $17 for the strike price, and then pay the premium on this. You then may also get this at the money, which means you're basically buying this at $15 since that's the current price of this on the market.

So, how is this financed? Well, the premium that was used on purchasing the previous call options is the answer to that. The investor in this will sell the option that's either in the money or below this, so you may sell an option or $13 when the current price is $15 and then buy the $17 for himself.

So what does that do for you well, selling this the investor will then get a credit for the premium on this, and it offsets the cost of this, and it will help pay for this, but of course, the premiums of this does change due to the volatility of the stock market and the like as well.

Again, the purpose of this is unlimited profit with limited risk on this, and essentially, it's taken when the underlying stock will also experience a significant change, but it's mostly in the upside in the future. When it does so, the investor will then be able to make money off of that. It essentially is allowing the investor to pay for the current stock, and then taking that money that he made, getting an option, and when that expires and say the stock goes higher than it was before, then the investor can cash in on that option. At that point they can do whatever they want with it, whether that be a covered call, or whatever they feel is necessary.

Now this is a backspread strategy, and we'll go over another one very shortly, but the purpose of this is to benefit from the trend reversals, or significant movements or changes in the market. Strategies that involve the backspread that's call ratio are part of a category called strategies for ratios, which the goal of this is to own call options on this because the investor thinks it will go up. The price will then compensate for the premium paid, but the sale of the option that's in the money helps offset this.

Let's look at an example So you've got stock X, which is trading for $43 in June, and an options trader decides to execute a backspread by selling one JUL40 call, for $400, and two JUL 45 calls, each for 200, and then, they take that and put it in there. You notice that it's trading at

$45, but then the JUL45 option is worthless, but the short JUL40 call is then within the money, which means that it gets $500 in intrinsic value, so if you buy back this call in order to close the position, the trader will get the max loss of $500 on this. But, let's say that it's trading at $50 on this, and all of these options expire in the money. The short is now worth $100 on this, and it needs to be brought back to close that. Since the other two JUL45 calls bought are now $500 on this, you're getting the combined value together of $100, and that's enough to offset the losses from the call that's written, so the person achieves the breakeven point of only $50. But, beyond that though, no losses are incurred. But what if the stock jumps to $60, which is a significant increase, and you then have a JUK45 stock that's worth $1500, and then the single JUL40 stock will be $2000, which results in a $1000 profit. So you should consider all of these options, and the best thing about this is that if you are familiar with how the market moves, you can come out of this on top.

Investors using this will sell the calls at a much lower strike price, and buy more at a higher strike price, and the most common ratios is uses two out of the money with three in the money, and the strategy is established at a credit, s the trader will get a small gain if the price of the stock decreases a lot. This is the type of trading that benefits when the market is volatile since investors typically will use this when they believe that the markets are supposed to move higher. By buying and selling these call options, you can hedge the downside risk, while benefitting from the upside as the markets begin to gain, and backspread strategies are used on a standalone basis, and to "go long" within the market, or they can be used as a more complex investing position.

This is used in a more bullish market too, so remember that before you begin with this type of trading.

The Put Ratio backspread

On the flipside, let's take the put ratio backspread, which essentially combines short puts and long puts in order to create a position that has a profit and loss potential that's dependent on the ratio of the puts that are there. The put ratio backspread is called this, since the volatility of the stock is essentially how it profits, and it works to create unlimited profit potential with limited loss, and limited profit potential with the prospect of unlimited loss, which is dependent on how it is structured.

Now this strategy is one of the more unusual ones, where you are selling an at-the-money short put in order to pay for an extra out-of-the-money long put. You essentially want to establish this with a small net credit when you can, so that if you're dead wrong, you can still make a small profit, depending on the conditions, the expiration of the days, and the distance between this.

You want to use this ideally with longer options, in order to give the stock time to move, but the marketplace isn't dumb, so you should know that the further that you go, the more likely you'll need to establish your strategy for a debit. The further the strikes are apart too, the more of a strategy for a credit that you have to put in, but of course, that's a tradeoff.

The more you increase the distance between these strike prices, the much bigger the risk since the stock will have to make a bigger move to the downside so that you don't lose. If the stock only makes a small move to the downward side, you'll suffer a lot more loss, but that's only looking at expiration, not beforehand. So, if it does move towards the strike price of the stock that you bought, it will be profitable. You should know that these are going to be adversely affected by time decay too, so you should make sure that the stock is acting bearish when moving in order to make this profitable.

So what's an example of this? Well, the put ratio backspread uses both short and long puts in order to for it to form the volatility of the stock. Now, the stock needs to be going down and be volatile in a downward manner for it to be profitable.

Here is another example. Let's you have a stock that's trading in currently at $29.50, and it may have a one-month put that goes with a $30 put trading at $1.16, or a $29 that is trading at 62 cents. A trader who is bearish on the stock will want to have a backspread that profits from the decline, so it will buy two of those $29 put contracts, which will only cost you $124, and from there, put the $30 for sale and receive the premium of $116 on there. You then may have to take commissions into account, which is $8. so let's say the stock does decline to $28 when it expires, and the trade breaks even, which only costs the investor

96

$8 at the time of the trade. Now, let's say it falls to $27, the gain is then $100, and then, when it goes to $26, the gross gain is about $200, and from there, you're making more and more. So if the stock tanks, you're profiting. This is especially good if you know that there is a chance it's going to go down.

However, let's say that the stock goes up to $30. You may wonder at this point how much you're going to lose, but there's the reality of it: you're only going to lose $8. Not a lot of loss, right? Well, even if the stock climbs somehow to $40, you're only losing $8, which is a much lower profit loss than what it could be.

This type of spread is one that you should study and know what you're doing before you can do this type of trading. That is because usually, you need to know which stocks to sell in order to get a profit, and which ones to buy, and the strike price that will net you a profit. You should spend a little bit of time looking at market trends, and only attempt this in a bearish market. In contrast, call ratio backspreads should only be accomplished when there is a more bullish market. We'll go over what each of those types of markets is, and how they can benefit traders in the next chapter.

The Butterfly Spread-Long Put Butterfly

Now we have the butterfly spread, which includes multiple types of spreads. For the most part, we'll be focusing on the long put butterfly, but we will also touch on what exactly the butterfly spread is, and why they matter.

Butterfly spreads essentially combine both the bull and the bear spreads, which essentially has a fixed risk and total profit. This uses four different contracts but three different strike prices, one that is higher, one that is at the strike price currently, and only with a lower strike price, with the same distance from the at-the-money option. For example, if you have a strike price that's $60, the three options are $65, $60, and $55, respectively. So essentially, you're doing it within $5 of one another. You can use puts and calls on this and combining each of these different options creates different types of butterfly spreads, each of which profits from volatility, or lower volatility.

So you've got the long put butterfly spread, which is created by buying one that's at a lower than the strike price you have currently, having two that are sole at-the-money, and then buying one with a higher strike price, with the debit created by entering this. The one has a max profit when the underlying strike price is within these options in the middle. The max profit of this is the higher strike price minus the strike of the put that's sold, minus the premium paid. The max loss of the trade is limited to the commissions paid, and the premiums that you paid initially.

So the goal of this is to profit from the neutral strike price of the short puts, with limited risk.

Here is an example of this. You're essentially creating a three-part strategy that's created by buying one put at a higher strike price, two at lower, and then buying one lower, and they all have the same expiration date, and they're equidistant. To start, you buy a put at 6.25 premium for 105, and then you sell two at 100 for 3.15, and from there, you buy a put at 1.25 for the 95 strike price. You essentially want the market to stay near a certain level, and from there, you'll get a net cost. Now, you want to make sure that the stock is equal to the strike price of the center puts, so in this case, you want to hit the 100 in this case, or around it. If it goes above or below the two ends of this, you're losing out on money.

At this point let's say it goes up to 110 or 90, then you're losing money. But if it stays at say, 101, or 98, you're going to be in the money. This is definitely a more advanced strategy, since the profit potential is smaller, and the costs are high, and since you're working with three different strike prices, you're dealing with multiple commissions in addition to the three spreads that you have when you open up, and from there, close it. You want to make sure the prices are "good," and the risk/reward ratio on this is acceptable for what you're going for too.

The max profit is essentially the difference between the higher and center strike price, minus the cost of the premiums, and the profit is realized when the strike price is equal to the strike prices on this. The difference between the strike prices in the last example was $5, and the net cost of this was $1.20, not taking commissions into effect, so the max profit is $3.80, or $380, not including the commission, which is still good.

At this point, the max loss essentially happens when it goes above, or below. If the stock hits the highest strike price or above it, it makes all of the puts worthless, and the cost of the strategy is lost, but if it goes below the lowest strike price, all of the money is then at a net value of zero, and your max loss is whatever you paid for those premiums.

Breakeven is essentially the highest strike price and the lowest strike price. So if it does hit 105, like in the example above, you're getting the breakeven. And if it hits 95, you'll also hit the breakeven point.

Essentially, you want to make sure that you see a market that is either bearish or neutral, depending on the relationship of the stock price to the center strike price when this is established. If the strike price is near the center strike price, then the forecast is mostly unchanged, but if it does hit the center strike price, or is above it, then the forecast must be for it to fall.

Basically, you don't want a ton of volatility with this type of strategy.

Trading Options with ETFs

ETF or ETF options are essentially mutual funds that trade just like stocks, so at this point, any time during a trading day, investors can buy or even sell ETF that represents or tracks the market segments. Most of the ETFs that are there are good for investors to take advantage of. Many of them use long or short put options and leveraged positions in these types of securities. Foreign and domestic stock, currencies, physical commodities, financial assets, and bonds are all examples of ETF. They have many different options trading volumes, but most of them attract very little attention.

The most common ETFs that are traded are the SPDR Trust, the PowerShares QQQ Trusts, the iShares Russel 2000 Index Fund, and the SPDR Dow Jones Industrial Average.

ETFs are considered in many volumes is that they track the indexes that straight index options track, so you should look as well as the liquidity of the option as well.

Trading options on ETFs can result in the need to deliver shares on this, but index options may not have the same instance to it. The American options are also subject to "early exercise," which means they are often exercised before expiration, which triggers a trade of the security under this. Index options are bought and sold before expiration, but they can't be exercised.

With ETF options, up to the expiration date of the call, they have a right to get the underlying ETF at a certain price. For example, if you get an Oil ETF, you have a right to buy that for a certain price up to that point, but if the price never gets above the price that it was before, it will expire in a worthless manner. The price of these also varies as well, and you can protect or expose yourself by getting a call, depending on what you get.

When trading these ETFs, you need to pay attention to the bid-ask spread. Essentially, that's the difference between the buying price and the asking price, and typically, smaller spreads are better. You should look at the performance, tracking error, concentration, and the premium/discount on these in the spread. You should look at the different values of this and look to see how thin the spread can go.

As we also mentioned before, ETFs are liquid, which means that they are easily bought and sold. Of the 1800 Efts out there, about 1350 of these trade at a low volume, so you should understand how liquid the ETF is since this can limit the limit orders used. They are a valuable tool that's traded in securities, where even smaller orders have the potential to represent a high percentage of the ETF's daily average, and it impacts the prevailing market price. You should make sure that you control the execution price. If you get a buy limit order below the asking price, you want to get it for just under what you're going to sell it for.

Finally, if you do consider trying to trade these types of options, you will want to make sure that you avoid trading during the time the market opens and closes. Why is that? Well, there is more potential for increased volatility in the price, and you may want to consider trading at some of these times. You may not be able to see the difference in price, and this can, in turn, be overwhelming. You should try to make sure that you watch the market, and look at the spreads, in order to see what you can trade, and when you can.

When it comes to advanced strategies, these are something that you might not use right away, for the sole reason of, you don't really need to use them yet. But, if you're considering getting deeper into the realm of options trading, this is something that can be used to help you with getting a lot more out of this. You can always consider these over time as you build your portfolio and want to increase your profits on these strategies as well.

Knowing your Markets

Finally, let's talk bear and bull markets in options trading. Both are incredibly important to understanding how to utilize options, and here, we'll discuss the market trends, and why they matter, including some tips to help you with this.

The Bear Market

Bear markets are essentially the first part of this that we are going to talk about, and it's essentially when there is a general decline in the market over a period of time. Bear markets will typically swing high investor optimism, to both fear, and pessimism.

There is also a mentality that goes along with this, which is where the market or the stock will drop in value. Bear markets expect it to decline, and from there, sell the commodity at a lower price, which is more speculation in that sort of way. The market typically is more gradually declining, and then will become bullish once again.

Typically, the price of these securities falls about 20% or more from the highest, and usually, the general sentiment is negative. These usually have an association with the declines in an overall market, but usually, the securities are considered on a more individual level if it's a decline of 20% or more over a period of time, at least 2 months or more. The

US major market indexes actually fell into a bear market level back during Christmas time of last year. The longest prolonged bear market before that point was between 2007 and 2009, which was during the financial crisis, a time that, if you heard about the housing investment crisis, may be pretty familiar with it. During that time, it actually lost about 50% of the value, and investors weren't all that happy with it.

There are different types of bear markets too, and the biggest thing to remember is that these can actually fall into a much longer prolonged pattern, lasting anywhere from 10-20 years, characterized by a below average return that happens on a sustainable level. So, if it is a below average market, but it's a much more prolonged bias on all of this. This also may cause rallies to happen for a long period of time, since the gains aren't sustained, and the prices revert to the lower levels once again. In contrast, there are cyclical bear markets that last anywhere from a couple of weeks to many years.

Typically, the market will fall to a "market bottom" which is when it gets to the lowest point, signaling the end of the downturn, and the beginning of the upward trend of moving towards a more bullish market.

The problem with this is that while the bottom is reachable, it's very hard to identify what the bottom is, while this is happening. The same can go with a bullish market and the upturn, which we will get to in a minute.

But, the problem is, if you fall into the trap of assuming that the market bottom is at one point, and it turns out to be "false" it actually can cause you to lose profit trying this since you're selling it for lower prices than what you care to utilize.

Now, let's talk a bull market, and from there, discuss how you can look into potentially predicting these trends.

Bull markets

In complete contrast, you have the bull market, which is the market where the securities are rising, and they expect to rise. This is often used in the stock market but can be used for bonds, real estate, currencies, and other commodities. Because the prices of these essentially rise and fall during this, bull markets are essentially the trend of the prices for this rising, and they can last months, or in some cases years as well.

Bull markets are characterized by confidence, optimism, and the expectations that stronger results should continue for an extended period of time. It's difficult to predict it with the trends in the market, and part of the difficulty is the psychology of the speculation, and how it plays a part in this. There isn't a specific metric that identifies a bull market, unfortunately, but one of the most common characteristics is that the stock prices rise at least 20%, with it following after a drop of 20%, so typically the market goes into a bear form before it becomes bull. Since bull markets are hard to predict, usually, this happens. The most notable bull market is between 2003-2007, which is actually right after a decline, but then, after a bit, the 2008 financial crisis hit, and from there, it hit the market with major declines, but again, this was right after a bull market happened. So, it goes bear, then bull, and then bear once more, following this pattern appropriately.

Bull markets tend to happen when the economy is strong, or it's already growing strong, and it happens when the GDO and the unemployment rates are good, and there is a rise in profits on a corporate level, with more demand for stocks generally. It helps with the overall tone of the market too, and it increases the IPO activity during this time. It also is much more quantifiable in measurement than others. Some of the other factors in this are hard to quantify though, since supply and demand does still seesaw in this case. Many are eager to get securities, and investors are more than willing to get rid of their stock in order to gain profits. There is much more happening with how the market goes around, and the transactions are done, and many people are trading during this point.

Essentially, these do coincide with the economic cycle, which goes through phases of expansion, peaking, contraction, and then the trough, which is the lowest point. It involves a lot more economic expansion, since public sentiment about the economic conditions does drive the stock a little bit, and the prices tend to rise much higher than they did before. Bear markets usually happen right before a contraction economically happens, such as the recession happening right before a large and expanding stock market.

Trading in Bear Markets

So to profit in bear markets, investors do look at taking short positions or short selling, which is when you borrow and anticipate it to fall once again. This, in turn, will allow you to cover a position that you're profiting on. You can from there buy back the shares to close it out, profiting from the fall. Short positions are extremely risky though, with unlimited potential losses. I would recommend against shorting stocks in a bear market.

Put options are your best friend, and essentially that is because you're giving the right to sell something at a strike price in the future. The money you pay is a premium, and put options increase when the stock falls, so it makes sense to use this in a bear market. If it falls below the strike price, you can then sell it at the higher price, or sell it completely for profit.

You should also consider short ETFs, which is essentially the returns that are inverse of the index. If you decide to trade a stock that performs inverse on Nasdaq 100, about 25%, it will then later on rising above 25%, and raises itself proportionally. The inverse relationship is good for those who want to profit when the market is downturned, or who want to hedge the long positions against this, in turn making sure that they get a profit.

Basically, you want to trade with the idea of profiting in a falling market.

Trading in Bull Markets

If you want to benefit from a bull market, you need to buy early to take advantage of their rising prices, and from there wait to sell them when they reach the peak price. However, it is hard to determine how to go about this, but there are a few ways to do this.

First and foremost, you want to consider going along with your positions. Wait a bit, and you can always buy and hold, which is buying a security, holding onto it, and then selling it later on. This brings about more confidence for the investor, and it will allow you to look at market trends, and then trade and sell when the time is right.

Also, consider getting a long position, since it will let you profit the longer it's happening. You also want to exercise call options, since that gives you the right to buy the stock at the time. Calls go up when the value of the stock rises. If the stock rises past the strike price, the person can buy it, but you can actually still consider writing these, and still continue to rite these and make a profit since you can keep the stock above the strike price, and let it continue that.

Finally, you want to consider long ETFs, which allow you to have low transaction costs and operating expenses. They replicate the movement of the indexes followed, fewer expenses. For example, if the stock rises by 10%, the ETF then will rise by the same amount.

Finally, you want to consider retracement additions, which is a period in which the trend in the security is reversed, and even during bull markets, it's unlikely that it will only ascend. You want to look for retracements within this, and presume that if the market does continue, it will move up, and provide the investor with a discounted price.

How to Spot these Markets

The truth is, it's very hard to predict these, and some believe that predicting these is the key to investing, but it isn't that easy for you to do. Many will sell in bear markets since they don't want to risk the bigger losses at this point.

The best way to trade in these types of markets is to look at the cycle the market is in since investors will experience both of these, and the key is to profit when these are doing well, and when they are bottoming too. Yes, you can profit in a bottoming market, that's for sure. You also should consider the advance/decline line, which represents the advancing issues that are divided by the number of declining issues over time. A number greater than 1 is bullish, and less than 1 is bearish. A rising line means the markets are indeed getting higher, but declining line means that there is a chance that there is a bearish market, but it could also correct itself over time.

Now, the advance/decline line essentially shows the number where the stocks are advancing, or declining. If you see that it's exceeding the declines, it definitely will have a positive number to it. If you notice that the declines are exceeding the advances, it's a declining line. This shows the amount of times when a stock is falling.

If the number is greater than 1, it's advancing, but if it's less, it's declining, and traders can use this in order to plot the performance of a stock, and also compare it with the overall performance of a stock. If you see divergences, whether bearish or bullish, this is a chance that it might have a reversal and is a sign of it.

If it's been declining for a few months, but the averages are higher than usual, this is a negative correlation, and that usually means that a bear market is happening. The advance/decline line that continues to move down shows that the averages are weak, but if it rises again for a few months, and then the averages are moved down, it creates a positive divergence, which means that bull markets are starting to form, so it may be in your best interest to potentially trade in that market.

This is probably your best tool since it helps with determining trends and making it work.

If you notice that there are investors acting fearful and pessimistic during bear markets, a lot of times they'll fall into the trend of "panic selling" which is when they sell their shares in a panic. But, if you notice that there is more happening during a bull market, it involves more liquidity, higher trading volumes, and further raising of the stock prices.

Really, the best way to look at this, and to trade in each market is to look at the different advance/decline lines, look at the cycle, and from there, keep a portfolio that is incredibly diverse. Maintain enough liquidity in order to ride out the hard periods, so you don't have to resort to panic selling. Following this can help you prevent the worst from happening, and it can work to prevent this from getting worse over time, and in turn, make it easier for you to sell as well.

Conclusion

For many, options trading is the beginning of the future. We've gone over all of the nuances of options trading, but we have a few more things to talk to you about. Here, we'll dive into these last couple of tidbits, and some other helpful information to assist you with trades.

The Risks of Options Trading

There are risks to options trading that are worth mentioning, and here, we'll discuss what they are, and why these risks should be mentioned when looking at options trading.

The first is that options often expose sellers to more chances of loss. Unlike buyers or holders, the seller typically can incur a much greater loss than the contract price, because when you write a call or put, you're obligated to sell the shares at a price within a time frame. Even if it's not favorable to do so, and there isn't a cap on how high or how low the stock can go.

There is also a limited time for this investment to bear out. This is a short-term investment. Options traders are always looking to capitalize on a price movement in the short term, so it must take place within days, weeks, or months from when the price movement happens, or when the payoff happens. This means, you need to make the right assumptions, which means you are picking the right time to buy the option, and then deciding when you should exercise, sell, or just walk away before the option expires out. However, if you're a long-term investor you might have some benefits from this.

Also, one of the drawbacks is how you get started, and the transaction fees. In order to begin, you need broker approval, which means answering a bunch of questions about your finances, any experience you have with investing, and from there, any other experience and understanding of the risks. From there, you'll get the training level that you're allowed. You need to have minimally two grand in your brokerage account, so if you're not ready to take that on, you probably shouldn't be doing this kind of trading.

Plus, we also talked a little bit about the extra fees. Every transaction has a fee, but you might need to set up a margin account, and this is basically a credit line that's collateral in case you end up messing up a trade. Each of these brokerages has different levels and requirements for this, and it will base all of this on the rate of interest, and how much securities and cash are within the account. These can be pricey in some cases and rack up over time. If you're unable to make good on the loan, you may end up getting a margin call that will ultimately fully liquidate your account, basically stopping all of the trades, so you can't add more stocks or cash to it, and that in turn will increase all of these risks. You definitely will want to keep all of these in mind.

You probably won't get a lot of money from this right away, and you need to realize that if you're selling uncovered calls, it puts you even more at risk, so keep that in mind. Y

While there are many risks, though, understanding the different types of options that you have, and how to utilize them will help reduce the risk of every trade. Every single investment carries some risk, so you'll definitely want to make sure that you know about these and understand that you could potentially lose everything if you're not careful.

While options are safety nets, they aren't without risk, and because they are short-term, you need to be on the ball, and you should understand all of these different aspects of options trading before they are included within the portfolio.

How to be Careful

So, what is the best way to be careful? Well, first and foremost, there are a few ways to reduce your risk. If you're concerned that the price of shares of something is about to drop, you can get puts that give you the right to sell this at a strike price, no matter how low this drops. The investor essentially fortifies them against some levels of loss. This is called hedging, and we talked a little bit about this beforehand.

Hedging is also a way to mitigate risk, but it isn't the end-all to preventing this. Everything will have some form of a risk to it, and you should always make sure any prospect of hedging your portfolio in order to minimize the risk that comes with it. You should always understand your risks on this when you're trying to put together your portfolio.

Another way to protect yourself from   risk is to understand the options that you're going to invest in. If you're going to be successful, you need to know the ins and outs of a company, including what is going on, whether they're going to improve or decrease in value, and whether it would be best to do one type of trade or another. It also will help, especially if you're unsure of the total impact of this. You need to also know the intrinsic value of the company, and a solid idea of the business, and the trends that are there, including any big market trends that will affect this, and other macroeconomic impacts that come from this. Lots of times, investors don't need to make it needlessly complex, but you should definitely make sure that you understand the different risks to this type of trading and have a good idea of the basics before you take this any further.

Identifying the risks that come with every option is one of the key parts of options trading, and the biggest lesson you need to learn is controlling the risk with calls and puts, under the technicalities of the security. Look at each trade from every angle, to minimize the risk by protecting yourself with the spread strategies that were discussed in the previous chapters.

Those spreads are there to help you protect yourself. While spreads are a bit more complex than your average trade, when you're trying to reduce the risk, this is the way to do it..

You should always be concerned about two things: the exercising and the assignment. Exercising, of course, is when the person that has the option decides to cash in on it, where they essentially buy the stock that you have the option under. So you should make sure that you always have that. The second thing is the assignment, which is when you must fulfill the obligations of the options contract, which is when you essentially must deliver everything on the terms of the contract, and this is something that you should also keep in mind.

Now thankfully, only about 17-20% of options are exercised, but still, that's one in every five, and you should always be careful with this.

Spread strategies are probably one of the best things that you could learn as an options trader. You could focus on this, and you actually will profit with reducing the risk of it. You may wonder why traders don't use this, and usually, it's because the person doesn't understand it. Having these different trades and spreads at hand is actually a good way to protect yourself. Many don't know how to set them up and how to benefit from these trades. Once you understand these concepts, you'll realize you're actually near some serious opportunities that you should consider, and you'll realize there is a lot more that you can do than you think. Spread trading involves using the sale and making sure that you have the underlying security at different expiration dates, or in most cases a different strike price. So if you buy a call or put, you'll be bettering on whether or not it will go down, and you can focus more on the relationships of these options if you do end up using a spread.

You'll definitely have a lot more of an understanding of the market that you're looking into as well.

The other really important thing to do for yourself in this line of trading is education. Knowledge is power, and even more so in options trading. What many don't realize is that if they don't know something, they can end up losing out a lot on the trade. If you don't know a lot about how to reduce the risk of your trades, you'll definitely want to get more information. You can get a mentor, and they can help you through trades, or you can discuss it with your brokerage. A lot of these brokerages these days offer different services for those who are looking to make sure that they fully understand what they're getting into. Options trading is a bit complex, but you should know what you're doing before you begin.

Finally, always make sure that you know the break-even point for the option that you're purchasing. You need to know minimally what it takes in order to be profitable for you. You should look at the potential profits that you're going to get and figure out whether or not what you're buying is justified. If you notice that the trade isn't going to be worth it, then don't do it. Simple as that. You'll be amazed at how much of a difference this makes if you actually realize the potential of the trade. Many investors don't realize how much they're going to get from a trade, and it can end up biting them in the butt if they're not careful. The beauty of options trading is that you can control whether or not you're putting your money into it, whether or not you should buy the premiums, write those covered calls, or even put down a spread. You should educate yourself on market trends, and if you have questions, talk to others, since they may have been in the same situation that you were in before, and they can help.

Regardless of who you are, you should definitely understand the positions that you're in, what you are doing with your money, and the risks associated with this. This alone will help you succeed in the long term as a trader.

Successful Options Traders

There are successful traders out there who have made a lot of money off of this. Of course, some of these people have also made it big from just one trading period, and that's important to realize. Not all of them made it big just through options, but it's important to realize there are other different pools out there to jump into. Here are a few of the successful options traders that are out there.

Paul Tudor Jones is probably one of the most successful investors of all time, and he made his name over 30 years ago during the market crash back in 1987. He recognized that he should put down some put options in his portfolio. He did that, and during the Black Monday of 1987, he tripled his capital with those short positions. He did, later on, build the Tudor Investment Corp, which is a large $12 billion hedge fund that he is there, and while he is ranked #308 in the list of billionaires out there, he's still made a name for himself, which is pretty impressive.

Then there is George Soros, the man known for breaking the bank of England, and he is an options trader as well. A bulk of his portfolio is actually options trading. He had a large position in call options during the NYSE: SPY fund, and he actually had 9 million call options for SPY, which accounts to 16% of his portfolio, and he still has about 2.4 million of these put options, which basically lets him take control of both sides of the market. he's definitely holding both positions, no matter what happens. He's amassed a large amount of money over time, about $24.9 billion, and he's one of the wealthiest people in the world. He's one of the highest-ranked people on the Forbes self-made score, which is a very rare feat for most people.

There is also Edward Thorp, who is actually an interesting options trader. He's a mathematician that became a super successful author, and also became a hedge fund manager, which is probably why he is so good at watching the markets. He has written a lot of papers on options theory and has gotten a lot of remarkable returns. Those papers are available, and you can read them, and he's got a great knack for applying his understanding of statistics to the market at hand and exploited a lot of anomalies. He is a prime example of employing math to trading.

You also have Andy Kreifer, who is one of the best traders of all time, also capitalizing in the Black Monday crash during 1988. He used options, which were new at the time, in order to short the dollar in New Zealand. He shorted so many of these that his sell orders exceeded the supply of the money in New Zealand or the kiwi. It declined a lot, and Krieger actually netted about $300 million from this, and he even got a $3 million bonus for the efforts at hand, which is pretty astounding, don't you think?

Finally we have Blair Hull, who is also a lesser-known guru, but he was able to leverage the quantitative models and technology in order to make millions of dollars in options, futures, and equities in the ETF markets, and he spent a dozen years building a large trading company, selling it to Goldman Sachs back in 1999 for $531 million. He was bound by a non-compete clause; he ended up entering politics back in 2004, so he was a political figure for a while along with a very successful trader.

So, while it may take a very long time to get to that point, options trading is something that you should definitely consider. If you know your markets and know when to cash in on the markets, you'll be successful, and make some cash as well.

Resources for Options Traders

Options trading can be hard to learn, and if you feel like you need a little bit of assistance in options trading, there are options trading courses that you can try out.

Option Alpha is actually one of the best places to go to. First and foremost, there are 12 different courses here, and they're all free. You can work on these for 30 minutes every single day, and you can figure out the skills necessary in order to find out the ways to trade and get the best income. There are some great resources here, including how to understand pricing and volatility, earning trades, expirations, and more, and not only that, you can actually watch live videos of trades too. It's one of the best resources on the web! You can check here for more information: https://optionalpha.com/

Options Trading is another one to check out. It contains a lot of information on brokers, the basics of it, getting started, and how to improve. It even comes with some good brokers to check out, and you can start on your journey here. You can check here for more information: http://www.optionstrading.org/.

You also have **OptionsTradingIQ**, which is a site that offers a bunch of free tools that you can download from their site, including a worksheet to work out the trades that you want to utilize, profit tracking, management of different spreads and a trading plan, along with a trade evaluation worksheet. Basically, it gives you the knowledge that you need to make trades that you want to. You can access these free tools here: http://www.optionstradingiq.com/free-tools/.

Now let's talk about a paid option for this. There is the 3-course bundle on Udemy that is $12.99, and it discusses options trading and how to do it perfectly. There are over 11 hours of content for you to check out, and over 20K students have used it, so it's a worthwhile investment if you're looking to better understand. If you want to try a paid course, this is the way to go, and you can check it out here:

Finally, you have some books. Books are good, and usually, the content isn't going to change for the most part. But, **"Option as a Strategic Investment"** is probably your best book, to begin with, since it's actually deemed the "bible of options trading." This provides traders with the content that they need in order to minimize the risk and maximize the amount of profit that you have. There are over 1000 pages of content here, and you can figure out which works best, and you can also learn about tax laws here too. You'll get some advice on trading these too and measure the volatility of the market.

All of these different resources will help you become a trader or even a better trader, and you shouldn't just limit yourself to these options, but instead, learn to embrace all of these resources so you can and become the best trader possible.

If you've ever been curious about options trading, now is a great time to start. The best thing to do is begin slowly and work your way up so that you know what you're doing, and in turn, can create the best experience for yourself. If you have any questions, feel free to ask about them, and hopefully, this book provided the resources needed for your options trading adventures!

The end... almost!

Reviews are not easy to come by.

As an independent author with a tiny marketing budget, I rely on readers, like you, to leave a short review on Amazon.

Even if it's just a sentence or two!
So if you enjoyed the book, please head to the product page, and leave a review as shown below.

I am very appreciative for your review as it truly makes a difference.

Thank you from the bottom of my heart for purchasing this book and reading it to the end.

www.ingramcontent.com/pod-product-compliance
Lightning Source LLC
Chambersburg PA
CBHW071710210326
41597CB00017B/2423